THE PELICAN SHAKESPEARE
GENERAL EDITORS

STEPHEN ORGEL
A. R. BRAUNMULLER

Measure for Measure

An eighteenth-century Isabella: Mary Anne Yates
(1728–1787) at Drury Lane in the 1760s. Coached by
Garrick, she was praised for her severe dignity in the role. She
was considered the greatest tragic actress between the death of
Mrs. Cibber and the rise of Mrs. Siddons.

William Shakespeare

———

Measure for Measure

EDITED BY JONATHAN CREWE

PENGUIN BOOKS

PENGUIN BOOKS
Published by the Penguin Group
Penguin Group (USA) Inc., 375 Hudson Street, New York, New York 10014, U.S.A.
Penguin Group (Canada), 90 Eglinton Avenue East, Suite 700, Toronto, Ontario,
Canada M4P 2Y3 (a division of Pearson Penguin Canada Inc.)
Penguin Books Ltd, 80 Strand, London WC2R 0RL, England
Penguin Ireland, 25 St Stephen's Green, Dublin 2, Ireland
(a division of Penguin Books Ltd)
Penguin Group (Australia), 250 Camberwell Road, Camberwell, Victoria 3124,
Australia (a division of Pearson Australia Group Pty Ltd)
Penguin Books India Pvt Ltd, 11 Community Centre, Panchsheel Park,
New Delhi – 110 017, India
Penguin Group (NZ), 67 Apollo Drive, Rosedale, North Shore 0632, New Zealand
(a division of Pearson New Zealand Ltd)
Penguin Books (South Africa) (Pty) Ltd, 24 Sturdee Avenue,
Rosebank, Johannesburg 2196, South Africa

Penguin Books Ltd, Registered Offices: 80 Strand, London WC2R 0RL, England

Measure for Measure edited by R. C. Bald published in the
United States of America by Penguin Books 1956
Revised edition published 1970
This new edition edited by Jonathan Crewe published 2000

20

LIBRARY OF CONGRESS CATALOGING IN PUBLICATION DATA
Shakespeare, William, 1564–1616.
Measure for measure / William Shakespeare; edited by Jonathan Crewe.
p.   cm.—(The Pelican Shakespeare)
Includes bibliographical references.
ISBN 978-0-14-071479-1
1. Chastity—Drama.   2. Brothers and sisters—Drama.
3. Vienna (Austria)—Drama.   I. Crewe, Jonathan V.   II. Title.   III. Series.
PR2824.A2 C74   2000
822.3'3—dc21   00-033661

Printed in the United States of America
Set in Adobe Garamond
Designed by Virginia Norey

Contents

Publisher's Note

IT IS ALMOST half a century since the first volumes of the Pelican Shakespeare appeared under the general editorship of Alfred Harbage. The fact that a new edition, rather than simply a revision, has been undertaken reflects the profound changes textual and critical studies of Shakespeare have undergone in the past twenty years. For the new Pelican series, the texts of the plays and poems have been thoroughly revised in accordance with recent scholarship, and in some cases have been entirely reedited. New introductions and notes have been provided in all the volumes. But the new Shakespeare is also designed as a successor to the original series; the previous editions have been taken into account, and the advice of the previous editors has been solicited where it was feasible to do so.

Certain textual features of the new Pelican Shakespeare should be particularly noted. All lines are numbered that contain a word, phrase, or allusion explained in the glossarial notes. In addition, for convenience, every tenth line is also numbered, in italics when no annotation is indicated. The intrusive and often inaccurate place headings inserted by early editors are omitted (as is becoming standard practice), but for the convenience of those who miss them, an indication of locale now appears as the first item in the annotation of each scene.

In the interest of both elegance and utility, each speech prefix is set in a separate line when the speaker's lines are in verse, except when those words form the second half of a verse line. Thus the verse form of the speech is kept visually intact. What is printed as verse and what is printed as prose has, in general, the authority of the original texts. Departures from the original texts in this regard have only the authority of editorial tradition and the judgment of the Pelican editors; and, in a few instances, are admittedly arbitrary.

The Theatrical World

Economic realities determined the theatrical world in which Shakespeare's plays were written, performed, and received. For centuries in England, the primary theatrical tradition was nonprofessional. Craft guilds (or "mysteries") provided religious drama – mystery plays – as part of the celebration of religious and civic festivals, and schools and universities staged classical and neoclassical drama in both Latin and English as part of their curricula. In these forms, drama was established and socially acceptable. Professional theater, in contrast, existed on the margins of society. The acting companies were itinerant; playhouses could be any available space – the great halls of the aristocracy, town squares, civic halls, inn yards, fair booths, or open fields – and income was sporadic, dependent on the passing of the hat or on the bounty of local patrons. The actors, moreover, were considered little better than vagabonds, constantly in danger of arrest or expulsion.

In the late 1560s and 1570s, however, English professional theater began to gain respectability. Wealthy aristocrats fond of drama – the Lord Admiral, for example, or the Lord Chamberlain – took acting companies under their protection so that the players technically became members of their households and were no longer subject to arrest as homeless or masterless men. Permanent theaters were first built at this time as well, allowing the companies to control and charge for entry to their performances.

Shakespeare's livelihood, and the stunning artistic explosion in which he participated, depended on pragmatic and architectural effort. Professional theater requires ways to restrict access to its offerings; if it does not, and admission fees cannot be charged, the actors do not get paid, the costumes go to a pawnbroker, and there is no such thing as a professional, ongoing theatrical tradition. The answer to that economic need arrived in the late 1560s and 1570s with the creation of the so-called public or amphitheater playhouse. Recent discoveries indicate that the precursor of the Globe playhouse in London (where Shakespeare's mature plays were presented) and the Rose theater (which presented Christopher Marlowe's plays and some of Shakespeare's earliest ones) was the Red Lion theater of 1567. Archaeological studies of the foundations of the Rose and Globe theaters have revealed that the open-air theater of the 1590s and later was probably a polygonal building with fourteen to twenty or twenty-four sides, multistoried, from 75 to 100 feet in diameter, with a raised, partly covered "thrust" stage that projected into a group of standing patrons, or "groundlings," and a covered gallery, seating up to 2,500 or more (very crowded) spectators.

These theaters might have been about half full on any given day, though the audiences were larger on holidays or when a play was advertised, as old and new were, through printed playbills posted around London. The metropolitan area's late-Tudor, early-Stuart population (circa 1590-1620) has been estimated at about 150,000 to 250,000. It has been supposed that in the mid-1590s there were about 15,000 spectators per week at the public theaters; thus, as many as 10 percent of the local population went to the theater regularly. Consequently, the theaters' repertories – the plays available for this experienced and frequent audience – had to change often: in the month between September 15 and October 15, 1595, for instance, the Lord Admiral's Men performed twenty-eight times in eighteen different plays.

Since natural light illuminated the amphitheaters' stages, performances began between noon and two o'clock and ran without a break for two or three hours. They often concluded with a jig, a fencing display, or some other nondramatic exhibition. Weather conditions determined the season for the amphitheaters: plays were performed every day (including Sundays, sometimes, to clerical dismay) except during Lent – the forty days before Easter – or periods of plague, or sometimes during the summer months when law courts were not in session and the most affluent members of the audience were not in London.

To a modern theatergoer, an amphitheater stage like that of the Rose or Globe would appear an unfamiliar mixture of plainness and elaborate decoration. Much of the structure was carved or painted, sometimes to imitate marble; elsewhere, as under the canopy projecting over the stage, to represent the stars and the zodiac. Appropriate painted canvas pictures (of Jerusalem, for example, if the play was set in that city) were apparently hung on the wall behind the acting area, and tragedies were accompanied by black hangings, presumably something like crepe festoons or bunting. Although these theaters did not employ what we would call scenery, early modern spectators saw numerous large props, such as the "bar" at which a prisoner stood during a trial, the "mossy bank" where lovers reclined, an arbor for amorous conversation, a chariot, gallows, tables, trees, beds, thrones, writing desks, and so forth. Audiences might learn a scene's location from a sign (reading "Athens," for example) carried across the stage (as in Bertolt Brecht's twentieth-century productions). Equally captivating (and equally irritating to the theater's enemies) were the rich costumes and personal props the actors used: the most valuable items in the surviving theatrical inventories are the swords, gowns, robes, crowns, and other items worn or carried by the performers.

Magic appealed to Shakespeare's audiences as much as it does to us today, and the theater exploited many deceptive and spectacular devices. A winch in the loft above the stage, called "the heavens," could lower and raise actors playing gods, goddesses, and other supernatural figures to and from the main acting area, just as one or more trapdoors permitted entrances and exits to and from the area, called "hell," beneath the stage. Actors wore elementary makeup such as wigs, false beards, and face paint, and they employed pig's bladders filled with animal blood to make wounds seem more real. They had rudimentary but effective ways of pretending to behead or hang a person. Supernumeraries (stagehands or actors not needed in a particular scene) could make thunder sounds (by shaking a metal sheet or rolling an iron ball down a chute) and show lightning (by blowing inflammable resin through tubes into a flame). Elaborate fireworks enhanced the effects of dragons flying through the air or imitated such celestial phenomena as comets, shooting stars, and multiple suns. Horses' hoofbeats, bells (located perhaps in the tower above the stage), trumpets and drums, clocks, cannon shots and gunshots, and the like were common sound effects. And the music of viols, cornets, oboes, and recorders was a regular feature of theatrical performances.

For two relatively brief spans, from the late 1570s to 1590 and from 1599 to 1614, the amphitheaters competed with the so-called private, or indoor, theaters, which originated as, or later represented themselves as, educational institutions training boys as singers for church services and court performances. These indoor theaters had two features that were distinct from the amphitheaters': their personnel and their playing spaces. The amphitheaters' adult companies included both adult men, who played the male roles, and boys, who played the female roles; the private, or indoor, theater companies, on the other hand, were entirely composed of boys aged about 8 to 16, who were, or could pretend to be, candidates for singers in a church or a royal boys' choir. (Until 1660, professional theatrical companies included no women.) The playing space would appear much more familiar to modern audiences than the long-vanished amphitheaters; the later indoor theaters were, in fact, the ancestors of the typical modern theater. They were enclosed spaces, usually rectangular, with the stage filling one end of the rectangle and the audience arrayed in seats or benches across (and sometimes lining) the building's longer axis. These spaces staged plays less frequently than the public theaters (perhaps only once a week) and held far fewer spectators than the amphitheaters: about 200 to 600, as opposed to 2,500 or more. Fewer patrons mean a smaller gross income, unless each pays more. Not surprisingly, then, private theaters charged higher prices than the amphitheaters, probably sixpence, as opposed to a penny for the cheapest entry.

Protected from the weather, the indoor theaters presented plays later in the day than the amphitheaters, and used artificial illumination – candles in sconces or candelabra. But candles melt, and need replacing, snuffing, and trimming, and these practical requirements may have been part of the reason the indoor theaters introduced breaks in the performance, the intermission so dear to the heart of theatergoers and to the pocketbooks of theater concessionaires ever since. Whether motivated by the need to tend to the candles or by the entrepreneurs' wishing to sell oranges and liquor, or both, the indoor theaters eventually established the modern convention of the noncontinuous performance. In the early modern "private" theater, musical performances apparently filled the intermissions, which in Stuart theater jargon seem to have been called "acts."

At the end of the first decade of the seventeenth century, the distinction between public amphitheaters and private indoor companies ceased. For various cultural, political, and economic reasons, individual companies gained control of both the public, open-air theaters and the indoor ones, and companies mixing adult men and boys took over the formerly "private" theaters. Despite the death of the boys' companies and of their highly innovative theaters (for which such luminous playwrights as Ben Jonson, George Chapman, and John Marston wrote), their playing spaces and conventions had an immense impact on subsequent plays: not merely for the intervals (which stressed the artistic and architectonic importance of "acts"), but also because they introduced political and social satire as a popular dramatic ingredient, even in tragedy, and a wider range of actorly effects, encouraged by their more intimate playing spaces.

Even the briefest sketch of the Shakespearean theatrical world would be incomplete without some comment on the social and cultural dimensions of theaters and playing in the period. In an intensely hierarchical and status-conscious society, professional actors and their ventures had hardly any respectability; as we have indicated, to protect themselves against laws designed to curb vagabondage and the increase of masterless men, actors resorted to the near-fiction that they were the servants of noble masters, and wore their distinctive livery. Hence the company for which Shakespeare wrote in the 1590s called itself the Lord Chamberlain's Men and pretended that the public, money-getting performances were in fact rehearsals for private performances before that high court official. From 1598, the Privy Council had licensed theatrical companies, and after 1603, with the accession of King James I, the companies gained explicit royal protection, just as the Queen's Men had for a time under Queen Elizabeth. The Chamberlain's Men became the King's Men, and the other companies were patronized by the other members of the royal family.

These designations were legal fictions that half-concealed an important economic and social development, the evolution away from the theater's organization on the model of the guild, a self-regulating confraternity of individual artisans, into a proto-capitalist organization. Shakespeare's company became a joint-stock company, where persons who supplied capital and, in some cases, such as Shakespeare's, capital and talent, employed themselves and others in earning a return on that capital. This development meant that actors and theater companies were outside both the traditional guild structures, which required some form of civic or royal charter, and the feudal household organization of master-and-servant. This anomalous, maverick social and economic condition made theater companies practically unruly and potentially even dangerous; consequently, numerous official bodies – including the London metropolitan and ecclesiastical authorities as well as, occasionally, the royal court itself – tried, without much success, to control and even to disband them.

Public officials had good reason to want to close the theaters: they were attractive nuisances – they drew often riotous crowds, they were always noisy, and they could be politically offensive and socially insubordinate. Until the Civil War, however, anti-theatrical forces failed to shut down professional theater, for many reasons – limited surveillance and few police powers, tensions or outright hostilities among the agencies that sought to check or channel theatrical activity, and lack of clear policies for control. Another reason must have been the theaters' undeniable popularity. Curtailing any activity enjoyed by such a substantial percentage of the population was difficult, as various Roman emperors attempting to limit circuses had learned, and the Tudor-Stuart audience was not merely large, it was socially diverse and included women. The prevalence of public entertainment in this period has been underestimated. In fact, fairs, holidays, games, sporting events, the equivalent of modern parades, freak shows, and street exhibitions all abounded, but the theater was the most widely and frequently available entertainment to which people of every class had access. That fact helps account both for its quantity and for the fear and anger it aroused.

WILLIAM SHAKESPEARE OF
STRATFORD-UPON-AVON, GENTLEMAN

Many people have said that we know very little about William Shakespeare's life – pinheads and postcards are often mentioned as appropriately tiny surfaces on which to record the available information. More imaginatively and perhaps more correctly, Ralph Waldo Emerson wrote, "Shakespeare is the only biographer of Shakespeare. . . . So far from Shakespeare's being the least known, he is the one person in all modern history fully known to us."

In fact, we know more about Shakespeare's life than we do about almost any other English writer's of his era. His last will and testament (dated March 25, 1616) survives, as do numerous legal contracts and court documents involving Shakespeare as principal or witness, and parish records in Stratford and London. Shakespeare appears quite often in official records of King James's royal court, and of course Shakespeare's name appears on numerous title pages and in the written and recorded words of his literary contemporaries Robert Greene, Henry Chettle, Francis Meres, John Davies of Hereford, Ben Jonson, and many others. Indeed, if we make due allowance for the bloating of modern, run-of-the-mill bureaucratic records, more information has survived over the past four hundred years about William Shakespeare of Stratford-upon-Avon, Warwickshire, than is likely to survive in the next four hundred years about any reader of these words.

What we do not have are entire categories of information – Shakespeare's private letters or diaries, drafts and revisions of poems and plays, critical prefaces or essays, commendatory verse for other writers' works, or instructions guiding his fellow actors in their performances, for instance – that we imagine would help us understand and appreciate his surviving writings. For all we know, many such data never existed as written records. Many literary and theatrical critics, not knowing what might once have existed, more or less cheerfully accept the situation; some even make a theoretical virtue of it by claiming that such data are irrelevant to understanding and interpreting the plays and poems.

So, what do we know about William Shakespeare, the man responsible for thirty-seven or perhaps more plays, more than 150 sonnets, two lengthy narrative poems, and some shorter poems?

While many families by the name of Shakespeare (or some variant spelling) can be identified in the English Midlands as far back as the twelfth century, it seems likely that the dramatist's grandfather, Richard, moved to Snitterfield, a town not far from Stratford-upon-Avon, sometime before 1529. In Snitterfield, Richard Shakespeare leased farmland from the very wealthy Robert Arden. By 1552, Richard's son John had moved to a large house on Henley Street in Stratford-upon-Avon, the house that stands today as "The Birthplace." In Stratford, John Shakespeare traded as a glover, dealt in wool, and lent money at interest; he also served in a variety of civic posts, including "High Bailiff," the municipality's equivalent of mayor. In 1557, he married Robert Arden's youngest daughter, Mary. Mary and John had four sons – William was the oldest – and four daughters, of whom only Joan outlived her most celebrated sibling. William was baptized (an event entered in the Stratford parish church records) on April 26, 1564, and it has become customary, without any good factual support, to suppose he was born on April 23, which happens to be the feast day of Saint George, patron saint of England, and is also the date on which he died, in 1616. Shakespeare married Anne Hathaway in 1582, when he was eighteen and she was twenty-six; their first child was born five months later. It has been generally assumed that the marriage was enforced and subsequently unhappy, but these are only assumptions; it has been estimated, for instance, that up to one third of Elizabethan brides were pregnant when they married. Anne and William Shakespeare had three children: Susanna, who married a prominent local physician, John Hall; and the twins Hamnet, who died young in 1596, and Judith, who married Thomas Quiney – apparently a rather shady individual. The name Hamnet was unusual but not unique: he and his twin sister were named for their godparents, Shakespeare's neighbors Hamnet and Judith Sadler. Shakespeare's father died in 1601 (the year of *Hamlet*), and Mary Arden Shakespeare died in 1608 (the year of *Coriolanus*). William Shakespeare's last surviving direct descendant was his granddaughter Elizabeth Hall, who died in 1670.

Between the birth of the twins in 1585 and a clear reference to Shakespeare as a practicing London dramatist in Robert Greene's sensationalizing, satiric pamphlet, *Greene's Groatsworth of Wit* (1592), there is no record of where William Shakespeare was or what he was doing. These seven so-called lost years have been imaginatively filled by scholars and other students of Shakespeare: some think he traveled to Italy, or fought in the Low Countries, or studied law or medicine, or worked as an apprentice actor/writer, and so on to even more fanciful possibilities. Whatever the biographical facts for those "lost" years, Greene's nasty remarks in 1592 testify to professional envy and to the fact that Shakespeare already had a successful career in London. Speaking to his fellow playwrights, Greene warns both generally and specifically:

> . . . trust them [actors] not: for there is an upstart crow, beautified with our feathers, that with his tiger's heart wrapped in a player's hide supposes he is as well able to bombast out a blank verse as the best of you; and being an absolute Johannes Factotum, is in his own conceit the only Shake-scene in a country.

The passage mimics a line from *3 Henry VI* (hence the play must have been performed before Greene wrote) and seems to say that "Shake-scene" is both actor and play-wright, a jack-of-all-trades. That same year, Henry Chettle protested Greene's remarks in *Kind-Heart's Dream,* and each of the next two years saw the publication of poems – *Venus and Adonis* and *The Rape of Lucrece,* respectively – publicly ascribed to (and dedicated by) Shakespeare. Early in 1595 he was named as one of the senior members of a prominent acting company, the Lord Chamberlain's Men, when they received payment for court performances during the 1594 Christmas season.

Clearly, Shakespeare had achieved both success and reputation in London. In 1596, upon Shakespeare's application, the College of Arms granted his father the now-familiar coat of arms he had taken the first steps to obtain almost twenty years before, and in 1598, John's son – now permitted to call himself "gentleman" – took a 10 percent share in the new Globe playhouse. In 1597, he bought a substantial bourgeois house, called New Place, in Stratford – the garden remains, but Shakespeare's house, several times rebuilt, was torn down in 1759 – and over the next few years Shakespeare spent large sums buying land and making other investments in the town and its environs. Though he worked in London, his family remained in Stratford, and he seems always to have considered Stratford the home he would eventually return to. Something approaching a disinterested appreciation of Shakespeare's popular and professional status appears in Francis Meres's *Palladis Tamia* (1598), a not especially imaginative and perhaps therefore persuasive record of literary reputations. Reviewing contemporary English writers, Meres lists the titles of many of Shakespeare's plays, including one not now known, *Love's Labor's Won,* and praises his "mellifluous & hony-tongued" "sugred Sonnets," which were then circulating in manuscript (they were first collected in 1609). Meres describes Shakespeare as "one of the best" English playwrights of both comedy and tragedy. In *Remains . . . Concerning Britain* (1605),

William Camden – a more authoritative source than the imitative Meres – calls Shakespeare one of the "most pregnant witts of these our times" and joins him with such writers as Chapman, Daniel, Jonson, Marston, and Spenser. During the first decades of the seventeenth century, publishers began to attribute numerous play quartos, including some non-Shakespearean ones, to Shakespeare, either by name or initials, and we may assume that they deemed Shakespeare's name and supposed authorship, true or false, commercially attractive.

For the next ten years or so, various records show Shakespeare's dual career as playwright and man of the theater in London, and as an important local figure in Stratford. In 1608-9 his acting company – designated the "King's Men" soon after King James had succeeded Queen Elizabeth in 1603 – rented, refurbished, and opened a small interior playing space, the Blackfriars theater, in London, and Shakespeare was once again listed as a substantial sharer in the group of proprietors of the playhouse. By May 11, 1612, however, he describes himself as a Stratford resident in a London lawsuit – an indication that he had withdrawn from day-to-day professional activity and returned to the town where he had always had his main financial interests. When Shakespeare bought a substantial residential building in London, the Blackfriars Gatehouse, close to the theater of the same name, on March 10, 1613, he is recorded as William Shakespeare "of Stratford upon Avon in the county of Warwick, gentleman," and he named several London residents as the building's trustees. Still, he continued to participate in theatrical activity: when the new Earl of Rutland needed an allegorical design to bear as a shield, or *impresa,* at the celebration of King James's Accession Day, March 24, 1613, the earl's accountant recorded a payment of 44 shillings to Shakespeare for the device with its motto.

For the last few years of his life, Shakespeare evidently

concentrated his activities in the town of his birth. Most of the final records concern business transactions in Stratford, ending with the notation of his death on April 23, 1616, and burial in Holy Trinity Church, Stratford-upon-Avon.

THE QUESTION OF AUTHORSHIP

The history of ascribing Shakespeare's plays (the poems do not come up so often) to someone else began, as it continues, peculiarly. The earliest published claim that someone else wrote Shakespeare's plays appeared in an 1856 article by Delia Bacon in the American journal *Putnam's Monthly* – although an Englishman, Thomas Wilmot, had shared his doubts in private (even secretive) conversations with friends near the end of the eighteenth century. Bacon's was a sad personal history that ended in madness and poverty, but the year after her article, she published, with great difficulty and the bemused assistance of Nathaniel Hawthorne (then United States Consul in Liverpool, England), her *Philosophy of the Plays of Shakspere Unfolded.* This huge, ornately written, confusing farrago is almost unreadable; sometimes its intents, to say nothing of its arguments, disappear entirely beneath near-raving, ecstatic writing. Tumbled in with much supposed "philosophy" appear the claims that Francis Bacon (from whom Delia Bacon eventually claimed descent), Walter Ralegh, and several other contemporaries of Shakespeare's had written the plays. The book had little impact except as a ridiculed curiosity.

Once proposed, however, the issue gained momentum among people whose conviction was the greater in proportion to their ignorance of sixteenth- and seventeenth-century English literature, history, and society. Another American amateur, Catherine P. Ashmead Windle, made the next influential contribution to the cause when she published *Report to the British Museum* (1882), wherein she promised to open "the Cipher of Francis Bacon," though what she mostly offers, in the words of S. Schoenbaum, is "demented allegorizing." An entire new cottage industry grew from Windle's suggestion that the texts contain hidden, cryptographically discoverable ciphers – "clues" – to their authorship; and today there are not only books devoted to the putative ciphers, but also pamphlets, journals, and newsletters.

Although Baconians have led the pack of those seeking a substitute Shakespeare, in *"Shakespeare" Identified* (1920), J. Thomas Looney became the first published "Oxfordian" when he proposed Edward de Vere, seventeenth earl of Oxford, as the secret author of Shakespeare's plays. Also for Oxford and his "authorship" there are today dedicated societies, articles, journals, and books. Less popular candidates – Queen Elizabeth and Christopher Marlowe among them – have had adherents, but the movement seems to have divided into two main contending factions, Baconian and Oxfordian. (For further details on all the candidates for "Shakespeare," see S. Schoenbaum, *Shakespeare's Lives,* 2nd ed., 1991.)

The Baconians, the Oxfordians, and supporters of other candidates have one trait in common – they are snobs. Every pro-Bacon or pro-Oxford tract sooner or later claims that the historical William Shakespeare of Stratford-upon-Avon could not have written the plays because he could not have had the training, the university education, the experience, and indeed the imagination or background their author supposedly possessed. Only a learned genius like Bacon or an aristocrat like Oxford could have written such fine plays. (As it happens, lucky male children of the middle class had access to better education than most aristocrats in Elizabethan England – and Oxford was not particularly well educated.) Shakespeare received in the Stratford grammar school a formal education that would daunt many college graduates today; and popular rival playwrights such as the very learned Ben Jonson and George Chapman, both of whom also lacked university training, achieved great artistic success, without being taken as Bacon or Oxford.

Besides snobbery, one other quality characterizes the authorship controversy: lack of evidence. A great deal of testimony from Shakespeare's time shows that Shakespeare wrote Shakespeare's plays and that his contemporaries recognized them as distinctive and distinctly superior. (Some of that contemporary evidence is collected in E. K. Chambers, *William Shakespeare: A Study of Facts and Problems*, 2 vols., 1930.) Since that testimony comes from Shakespeare's enemies and theatrical competitors as well as from his co-workers and from the Elizabethan equivalent of literary journalists, it seems unlikely that, if any of these sources had known he was a fraud, they would have failed to record that fact.

Books About Shakespeare's Theater

Useful scholarly studies of theatrical life in Shakespeare's day include: G. E. Bentley, *The Jacobean and Caroline Stage*, 7 vols. (1941-68), and the same author's *The Professions of Dramatist and Player in Shakespeare's Time, 1590-1642* (1986); E. K. Chambers, *The Elizabethan Stage*, 4 vols. (1923); R. A. Foakes, *Illustrations of the English Stage, 1580-1642* (1985); Andrew Gurr, *The Shakespearean Stage*, 3rd ed. (1992), and the same author's *Play-going in Shakespeare's London*, 2nd ed. (1996); Edwin Nungezer, *A Dictionary of Actors* (1929); Carol Chillington Rutter, ed., *Documents of the Rose Playhouse* (1984).

Books About Shakespeare's Life

The following books provide scholarly, documented accounts of Shakespeare's life: G. E. Bentley, *Shakespeare: A Biographical Handbook* (1961); E. K. Chambers, *William Shakespeare: A Study of Facts and Problems*, 2 vols. (1930); S. Schoenbaum, *William Shakespeare: A Compact*

Documentary Life (1977); and *Shakespeare's Lives,* 2nd ed. (1991), by the same author. Many scholarly editions of Shakespeare's complete works print brief compilations of essential dates and events. References to Shakespeare's works up to 1700 are collected in C. M. Ingleby et al., *The Shakespeare Allusion-Book,* rev. ed., 2 vols. (1932).

The Texts of Shakespeare

As far as we know, only one manuscript conceivably in Shakespeare's own hand may (and even this is much disputed) exist: a few pages of a play called *Sir Thomas More*, which apparently was never performed. What we do have, as later readers, performers, scholars, students, are printed texts. The earliest of these survive in two forms: quartos and folios. Quartos (from the Latin for "four") are small books, printed on sheets of paper that were then folded twice, to make four leaves or eight pages. When these were bound together, the result was a squarish, eminently portable volume that sold for the relatively small sum of sixpence (translating in modern terms to about $5.00). In folios, on the other hand, the sheets are folded only once, in half, producing large, impressive volumes taller than they are wide. This was the format for important works of philosophy, science, theology, and literature (the major precedent for a folio Shakespeare was Ben Jonson's *Works*, 1616). The decision to print the works of a popular playwright in folio is an indication of how far up on the social scale the theatrical profession had come during Shakespeare's lifetime. The Shakespeare folio was an expensive book, selling for between fifteen and eighteen shillings, depending on the binding (in modern terms, from about $150 to $180). Twenty Shakespeare plays of the thirty-seven that survive first appeared in quarto, seventeen of which appeared during Shakespeare's lifetime; the rest of the plays are found only in folio.

The First Folio was published in 1623, seven years after Shakespeare's death, and was authorized by his fellow actors, the co-owners of the King's Men. This publication was certainly a mark of the company's enormous respect for Shakespeare; but it was also a way of turning the old plays, most of which were no longer current in the playhouse, into ready money (the folio includes only Shakespeare's plays, not his sonnets or other nondramatic verse). Whatever the motives behind the publication of the folio, the texts it preserves constitute the basis for almost all later editions of the playwright's works. The texts, however, differ from those of the earlier quartos, sometimes in minor respects but often significantly – most strikingly in the two texts of *King Lear,* but also in important ways in *Hamlet, Othello,* and *Troilus and Cressida.* (The variants are recorded in the textual notes to each play in the new Pelican series.) The differences in these texts represent, in a sense, the essence of theater: the texts of plays were initially not intended for publication. They were scripts, designed for the actors to perform – the principal life of the play at this period was in performance. And it follows that in Shakespeare's theater the playwright typically had no say either in how his play was performed or in the disposition of his text – he was an employee of the company. The authoritative figures in the theatrical enterprise were the shareholders in the company, who were for the most part the major actors. They decided what plays were to be done; they hired the playwright and often gave him an outline of the play they wanted him to write. Often, too, the play was a collaboration: the company would retain a group of writers, and parcel out the scenes among them. The resulting script was then the property of the company, and the actors would revise it as they saw fit during the course of putting it on stage. The resulting text belonged to the company. The playwright had no rights in it once he had been paid. (This system survives largely intact in the movie industry, and most of the playwrights of Shakespeare's time were as anonymous as most screenwriters are today.) The script could also, of course, continue to change as the tastes of audiences and the requirements of the actors changed. Many – perhaps most – plays were revised when they were reintroduced after any substantial absence from the repertory, or when they were performed by a company different from the one that originally commissioned the play.

Shakespeare was an exceptional figure in this world because he was not only a shareholder and actor in his company, but also its leading playwright – he was literally his own boss. He had, moreover, little interest in the publication of his plays, and even those that appeared during his lifetime with the authorization of the company show no signs of any editorial concern on the part of the author. Theater was, for Shakespeare, a fluid and supremely responsive medium – the very opposite of the great classic canonical text that has embodied his works since 1623.

The very fluidity of the original texts, however, has meant that Shakespeare has always had to be edited. Here is an example of how problematic the editorial project inevitably is, a passage from the most famous speech in *Romeo and Juliet,* Juliet's balcony soliloquy beginning "O Romeo, Romeo, wherefore art thou Romeo?" Since the eighteenth century, the standard modern text has read,

> What's Montague? It is nor hand, nor foot,
> Nor arm, nor face, nor any other part
> Belonging to a man. O be some other name!
> What's in a name? That which we call a rose
> By any other name would smell as sweet.
>   (II.2.40-44)

Editors have three early texts of this play to work from, two quarto texts and the folio. Here is how the First Quarto (1597) reads:

> Whats *Mountague?* It is nor hand nor foote,
> Nor arme, nor face, nor any other part.
> Whats in a name? That which we call a Rofe,
> By any other name would fmell as fweet:

Here is the Second Quarto (1599):

> Whats *Mountague?* it is nor hand nor foote,
> Nor arme nor face, ô be fome other name
> Belonging to a man.
> Whats in a name that which we call a rofe,
> By any other word would fmell as fweete,

And here is the First Folio (1623):

> What's *Mountague?* it is nor hand nor foote,
> Nor arme, nor face, O be fome other name
> Belonging to a man.
> What? in a names that which we call a Rofe,
> By any other word would fmell as fweete,

There is in fact no early text that reads as our modern text does – and this is the most famous speech in the play. Instead, we have three quite different texts, all of which are clearly some version of the same speech, but none of which seems to us a final or satisfactory version. The transcendently beautiful passage in modern editions is an editorial invention: editors have succeeded in conflating and revising the three versions into something we recognize as great poetry. Is this what Shakespeare "really" wrote? Who can say? What we can say is that Shakespeare always had performance, not a book, in mind.

Books About the Shakespeare Texts

The standard study of the printing history of the First Folio is W. W. Greg, *The Shakespeare First Folio* (1955). J. K. Walton, *The Quarto Copy for the First Folio of Shakespeare*

(1971), is a useful survey of the relation of the quartos to the folio. The second edition of Charlton Hinman's *Norton Facsimile* of the First Folio (1996), with a new introduction by Peter Blayney, is indispensable. Stanley Wells, Gary Taylor, John Jowett, and William Montgomery, *William Shakespeare: A Textual Companion,* keyed to the Oxford text, gives a comprehensive survey of the editorial situation for all the plays and poems.

THE GENERAL EDITORS

Introduction

IN SHAKESPEARE'S *Richard II*, King Richard replies to the English rebels who challenge his power by saying, "The breath of worldly men cannot depose / The deputy elected by the Lord" (III.2.56-57). In Richard's view, the divinely appointed king cannot lawfully be removed by his subjects. Indeed, as Richard sees it, his subjects cannot remove him lawfully or otherwise: no power on earth can do so. He is mistaken, of course, since he is deposed later in the play, but the position he claims as God's deputy was still the one generally claimed for kings and queens in the English monarchical theory of Shakespeare's time.

That position was asserted by King James I, the English ruler at the time *Measure for Measure* was written. Even before James came to power in 1603, he had polemically restated the case for divinely sanctioned royal authority in two books, *The True Law of Free Monarchies* (1598) and *Basilikon Doron* (1599). Both books were reissued in 1603, at the time of James's accession; the first recorded performance of *Measure for Measure* took place, almost concurrently, in 1604. Some lines from the introductory sonnet to *Basilikon Doron*, a book James couched as advice to his son and heir, Prince Henry, bear repetition in the context of *Measure for Measure*:

> If then ye would enjoy a happy reign
> Observe the statutes of your heavenly king,
> And from his law make all your laws to spring.
> Since his lieutenant here ye should remain,
> Reward the just; be steadfast, true and plain.

The nature and power of the lieutenant, or "deputy," as *Measure for Measure* has it, became the subject of prolonged, often ironic, exploration in Shakespeare's play.

Admittedly, the city of Vienna in *Measure for Measure* is no kingdom ruled over by an absolute monarch. Nor, for that matter, is it a Protestant realm, as was Shakespeare's England. It is a Catholic dukedom, and the clerical figures who move through it, including the duke when he goes into disguise, are friars. Yet Shakespeare makes little attempt at strict portrayal of a Viennese or a Catholic world. The suburbs where some brothels in the play are located belong to the geography of Shakespeare's London; there, "suburbs" were areas beyond city jurisdiction in which brothels could flourish – and so could theaters, including Shakespeare's – as they could not under strict city prohibition. Similarly, the play's exploration of "government" (I.1.3) belongs to Shakespeare's own time and place, as does its representation of a seamy, disease-ridden society. Certainly, the duke's understanding and exercise of power remain very close to those of James I's wished-for absolute monarchy. Although the duke begins the play by brushing aside abstract discussion of the "properties" (I.1.3) of government, those properties are precisely what the play will investigate.

When meditating on the character of the good ruler, for example, the duke says, "He who the sword of heaven will bear / Should be as holy as severe" (III.2.249-50). The bearer of heaven's sword is still god's deputy elect. Yet the duke in *Measure for Measure* feels sufficiently uncomfortable in his role as god's deputy to withdraw and deputize someone else in his place. The chosen deputy's deputy is Angelo, whose holy and severe demeanor recommends him. In the course of the play, Angelo deputizes Escalus in turn to execute some of his functions. Yet the duke is skeptical enough about pious appearances to retain control behind the scenes. He thereby places Angelo unwittingly on trial while reserving and masking his own position as deputy. It is from the duke's deputization of his own authority that the play's complicated action arises; the same act of deputization makes *Measure for Measure* a fascinating dramatized experiment in government by deputy. The mechanism under which any legitimate exercise of political and moral authority depends on a chain of "deputies," ultimately authorized by God as the supreme lawgiver, gets put to the test in *Measure for Measure.*

Of course, government works very differently in modern constitutional democracies from the way it worked in Shakespeare's England. Constitutional separations between church and state as well as legal distinctions between public and private domains had barely been instituted in Shakespeare's political world. Yet many of the questions posed in *Measure for Measure* about the nature and limits of state intervention and about the role(s) of those deputized to enforce the law remain current. In fact, late-twentieth-century readers continue to find *Measure for Measure* illuminating, not just about the general difficulty of legislating sexual morality, but about such matters as sexual harassment and blackmail by those in power. One of the play's central incidents – and, as we know, a persistent problem of "government" – concerns the powerful Angelo's offer to trade the condemned Claudio's life for sexual favors from Isabella. When Isabella threatens to expose him, Angelo confidently retorts, "Who will believe thee, Isabel?" (II.4.153). His high position will protect him, and his stainless reputation will make Isabella's charges seem incredible. It will be his word against hers. (Some recent criticism has addressed the severe penalties for "slander" that women invited if they chose to press charges of sexual impropriety against well-placed men during Shakespeare's time; in *Measure for Measure,* however, the "slanders" of which Angelo publicly accuses Isabella are vindicated when the duke exposes him.) What is unusual about the situation in the play is that we are able to witness an exchange of the kind to which there are seldom witnesses in real life. We know the truth about what happened; Angelo is clearly guilty as charged. Any general cultural predisposition to believe the powerful man rather than the woman under such circumstances is thus challenged by the play. Recognition of the play's continuing pertinence has, however, sometimes made *Measure for Measure* seem frustrating rather than satisfying to modern readers and audiences.

Rather than provide general philosophical solutions to the problems it poses, *Measure for Measure* delivers dramatic resolutions plotted according to Elizabethan conventions of romantic comedy ending in marriage. To many modern readers, the comedic happy ending of *Measure for Measure* evades the great issues of the play instead of resolving them in principle. Moreover, the play's grand finale, with marriages all round, has seemed forced, trivializing, problematic, or even sordid to many. For one of the characters, Lucio, forced marriage to a prostitute he has impregnated is a disgusting punishment – a fate worse than death – rather than a romantic reward. Whether marriage will amount to reward or punishment for the other couples involved remains uncertain. Perhaps, however, the play's forced and ambiguous resolution underlines the old dramatic truism that only God can write Act V. Although this duke *plays* God more than most stage characters do, and takes over the plotting of the play (perhaps that is one implication of being God's deputy), the solutions he delivers are no less flawed, theatrical, and conventional than he is. Not even the eye-for-an-eye poetic justice some readers crave is forthcoming. Angelo, who is practically condemned out of his own mouth and pleads for death, is "saved" instead for marriage by Mariana, whom he has previously repudiated. The play's happy ending is far removed from a perfect ending.

An uneasy fit between the dark, philosophical grandeur of *Measure for Measure* and comic devices some moderns have found disconcertingly cheap partly explains the play's classification in the twentieth century as a "problem comedy." (We have no evidence that Shakespeare's contemporaries would have regarded it as a problem.) Deputization, which seems central to the play's most serious concerns, reappears in seemingly frivolous contexts and parodic guises that some readers have found hard to take. Informal "deputization" in the play includes the duke's substitution of Mariana for Isabella in Angelo's bed (the time-honored bed trick of comedy) and the substitution of the dead pirate Ragozine's head for Claudio's. It includes the duke's substitution of yet another self for his own when he goes into disguise as a friar, a disguise in which he can undertake further impersonations, not the least of which is the impersonation of Death. (The fragmentation of the duke into other selves, and the consequent multiplication of his roles, defeats any attempt at integral character analysis.) Substitution – and substitutability – thus seems to emerge as the rule of the play. Why does it do so?

At least a part of the answer is that substitution is the general rule of theater. Actors are substituted for dramatic characters; men (or boy actors) for women, and vice versa; the dead for the living, and vice versa; sexual partners for one another; political functionaries for one another as well as for God. Alone among the characters in *Measure for Measure* (all of whom regard him as practically subhuman), the frequently dead-drunk Barnardine unwittingly resists the general rule of substitution when he refuses to be executed, thus withholding his head as a substitute for Claudio's. Yet even his surly refusal is circumvented when the head of a dead pirate is substituted for the one he declines to give up. In short, it is to a general rule of substitution that *Measure for Measure* owes its very existence as a play, and it is under the same rule that it produces its full range of effects, whether they strike us as dissonant or not. (Current "postmodern" readers and viewers of the play may in fact be more tolerant of dissonance, discrepancy, and parody than ones earlier in this century.) Where "all the world's a stage," as Jaques puts it in Shakespeare's *As You Like It,* substitution will be the rule.

The prehistory of the specific case to be considered under this general rule is outlined, mainly by the duke, at the beginning of the play. We are told that the citizens of Vienna, too long accustomed to lax regulation, have become morally dissolute and sexually licentious. The duke wishes to reimpose strict order, yet he feels that, having allowed things to slip, he cannot cruelly rein in his subjects himself. In this respect, the play echoes some of the language of *Basilikon Doron.* Warning against beginning a reign too tolerantly, James wrote, "And when ye have by the severity of justice once settled your countries, and made them know that ye can strike, then may ye after all the days of your life mix justice with mercy . . . for if otherwise ye kith [make known] your clemency at the first, the offenses would soon come to such great heaps [that you] against your nature would be compelled to wrack many whom the chastisement of few in the beginning might have preserved."* Shakespeare's duke accordingly appoints the austere Angelo to curb the citizens, investing him with full ducal powers. The duke then withdraws, ostensibly on a foreign mission but actually to become a disguised onlooker and manipulator of Angelo's rule.

Age-old questions about the appropriate degree of sexual regulation in society and about the relation between social and sexual order are thus implicitly raised at the beginning of the play. The implied norm to be policed under Angelo's rule is that of heterosexual marriage and procreation as the sole legitimate avenue of human sexuality. The first transgressor of whom Angelo decides to make an example is accordingly a young man, Claudio,

---

* James I, *Basilikon Doron,* ed. C. H. McIlwain (Cambridge: Harvard University Press, 1918): 20.

who has impregnated a young woman, Juliet, to whom he is only betrothed, not yet married. In sentencing Claudio to death, as Viennese law allows him to do, Angelo imposes a penalty that is not just unprecedented under the duke's rule but seems outrageously excessive to practically everyone but Angelo. For Angelo, however, enforcing the letter of the law – to which he believes he adheres in his own life – is the only way to begin an effective reform. Simultaneously with sentencing Claudio, Angelo attempts to close down all the Viennese brothels and severely penalize prostitutes and pimps. Angelo thus evidently regards organized prostitution as a cause and symptom of the same moral laxity for which Claudio is to be punished, and as a similar threat to marriage.

Ostensibly, Angelo's strict enforcement will uphold biblically prescribed moral and social norms, and will revive a respect for law and order that has been eroded through "liberty" (I.2.124). In other words, it will instill new terror into enforcement, needed to render the law effective. Angelo's enforcement may less overtly and perhaps only subconsciously be intended to promote public hygiene by limiting the spread of sexually transmitted disease, obviously rampant in Vienna. Yet we soon begin to glimpse Angelo's difficulties. Elbow the constable is a bumbling incompetent. Escalus, Angelo's deputy, is well-meaning but ineffectual. More damaging to Angelo's prospects, we learn, is the fact that brothels in the city, unlike those in the suburbs, have been saved by the intervention of a "wise burgher" (I.2.99). A political limit to Angelo's moral reform thus becomes evident; so does the fact that sex is a profitable free-market commodity with its own specialized providers. Public policy driven by moral concerns alone cannot overcome these brute facts. Moreover, when the bawd Pompey learns of Angelo's new policy of strict enforcement, he remarks that Angelo will have "to geld and splay all the youth of the city" (II.1.219-20). In effect, Pompey is making the self-serving claim that broth-els cater to the uncontrollable lust of young men, yet he has a point: not even savage penalties are enough to con-fine all youthful sexual activities within the bounds of marriage. The unavailing savagery of the penalties may in turn promote disrespect for the law. So must the transfor-mation of Pompey the bawd into an agent of the law when he is made assistant hangman. Ironically, Angelo himself will become the play's prime example of lawless-ness. Unexpectedly succumbing to his own desire for Is-abella, he will become the corrupter of the very law he has been deputized to uphold. All in all, Angelo's reforms have a great deal more to contend with than he antici-pates.

   Measure for Measure, then, seriously addresses issues of justice and law enforcement. Characters in the play, no-tably Angelo and Isabella, debate the issues with remark-able passion and eloquence. Yet the play as a whole reveals the huge gap between godlike aspirations and fallible human implementation. Indeed, the play goes further than I have already hinted in getting *behind* the wish for moral reform that drives the action. We are prompted to consider whether, or to what extent, the characters' moral rhetoric actually rationalizes and masks barely conscious sexual phobias arising from many causes: for example, from people's uneasy relation to their own sexuality (both its intensity and its "lawless" orientations); from the seemingly unbreakable link between human sexuality and human mortality (a connection underlined by jocular yet obsessive allusion in the play to sexually transmitted dis-eases); from various forms of sexual threat or abuse; from the deep sense of guilt regarding sex instilled by Christian tradition (even Claudio, who does not believe he has done anything terrible in impregnating Juliet, nevertheless feels sinful enough to reconcile himself, at moments, to a death sentence). All these phobia-inducing circumstances are sufficiently evident in the play to hint at an undercurrent of panic in its agendas of moral reform. Correspondingly, the play invites us to consider to what extent the incrimination of sexual offenders is a form of scapegoating for social and sexual "disorders" that can never fully be brought under control.

The institution of the prison in Vienna powerfully exemplifies both the penal impulse in the play and its limits. The existence of the prison implies a wish on the part of the authorities to cordon off – or internally exile – all threats to good order. Yet oscillation in the play between the social world of Vienna and its prison world reveals a failure to achieve this separation. The organized social world of the prison becomes an ironic reflection of the society in which it is situated, and a number of the characters cross the boundary between the two with only a change of role or costume. The social and prison worlds become increasingly interdependent, and the solution to the problems of the play depends on the mobility of characters across the supposedly dividing line.

Whatever we think of the solutions found in the play, they cannot possibly encompass all the circumstances, including unconscious ones, to which they respond. Such, perhaps, is one conclusion to be drawn from Shakespeare's study of "government," a term that increasingly throughout the play encompasses personal issues as well as explicitly political ones. Indeed, questions of public order and individual self-government remain interrelated throughout the play. When we first meet Isabella, she is seeking to enter a nunnery in which she can preserve her chastity and submit to regulation far stricter than that prevailing in Vienna (she even finds the convent rule somewhat too liberal for her taste). Her desire to enter the convent is an implied comment on the laxity of the Viennese social world and on the tainted selves – both bodies and souls – that it produces. The convent itself represents an attempt to cordon off an area of (female) purity from the contaminated city; what Isabella proposes for herself is internal exile from Vienna in a community of pure, strict, self-governing women. Her choosing to submit to strict discipline is an implicit defense of her inviolate self-hood, not just against the dissoluteness of the city, in which prostitution is rampant, but from lawful, patriar-chal marriage as a threat to women's autonomy and bod-ily intactness. Beyond even these motivations, the play suggests that Isabella's flight to the convent also represents an attempt on her part to separate herself from her brother Claudio, for whom she manifestly retains some incestuous sibling desire. Isabella's wish to enter the con-vent thus includes a phobic element of which she seems unaware; to feel secure, she wishes to substitute pure "sis-terhood" (I.4.5) for the cross-gendered sibling relation. Is-abella's retreat will soon be thwarted in the play when Lucio, who makes his way into the convent, urges her to plead with Angelo on behalf of Claudio. Isabella is thus drawn back into the world of compromising relation-ships, ultimately including marriage to the duke. Her concern for Claudio notwithstanding, Isabella's willing-ness to emerge from the convent she has just joined im-plies some ambivalence on her part about the cloistered life she has chosen.

Drawing on contemporary contexts, *Measure for Measure* supplies a particularly rich commentary on Isabella's impulse to withdraw. Although Catholicism continued to uphold ideals of chastity and cloistered virtue in Shake-speare's time, those ideals were relentlessly attacked and discredited by mainstream Protestants in England. In fact, English Catholic monasteries and convents had been dissolved during the reign of Henry VIII, while church property had been confiscated by the state. Virtuous mar-riage and procreation rather than celibate withdrawal were upheld as ideals for both men and women, though a double standard prevailed: more toleration was extended to men's transgressions. Isabella's initial decision to join a convent would have been regarded as questionable by many of Shakespeare's contemporaries; when the duke proposes marriage to her at the end of the play, he is offering her the "right" Protestant choice. (Different eras have responded differently to the fact that the text gives her no line accepting the offer, and in modern productions she has even occasionally refused it.)

The great English Puritan poet John Milton, in *Areopagitica,* definitively stated the English Protestant case in the seventeenth century. There, Milton discredited what he called "a fugitive and cloistered virtue," adding that "we bring not innocence into this world, we bring impurity much rather." In other words, the selves – and bodies – we would protect by walling out impurity already carry impurity within them; such is the meaning of original sin. The same point is graphically made in a poem called "Upon Appleton House" by Milton's contemporary Andrew Marvell; there, the Catholic nunnery is recalled as a fortified setting in which female vice and self-indulgence can flourish. Yet despite the force and persistence of the Protestant attack, cloistral ideals and impulses died hard. A long Catholic tradition did not end overnight in Protestant England. English Puritanism represented an attempt to redefine rather than wholly discredit religious aspirations to purity. Moreover, for both women and men, but perhaps more importantly for women, the cloistered life represented a rational alternative to the coercive norm of patriarchal marriage as well as to the sexual marketplace. This rational choice would no doubt have been phobically reinforced. Submitting to the rule of cloistered chastity (a choice sometimes entailing the rigors and ecstasies of martyrdom) was a paradoxical way of reclaiming self-determination in a "place apart." Shakespeare was not dealing with dead issues in *Measure for Measure.*

If Isabella represents the impulse to seek out a haven from the social world of the city, Mariana represents the corresponding danger to women of finding themselves relegated to an unchosen place apart. We hear that Mariana had been betrothed to Angelo, yet he had repudiated her when her dowry failed to come up to expectations. He additionally claims that her reputation had been tainted by rumors of sexual misconduct. She was therefore no longer fit to be his bride. Mariana is thus excluded from the marriage market, in which women's only opportunity for social inclusion resides, and she is confined to a "moated grange" (III.1.262), a place of exile from the life of the city. Mariana is the exemplary victim of a world in which adult single women have no place. Her isolation, which threatens to be perpetual, in a country house *outside* the city, makes the point. The duke recalls her only when she is needed as a substitute for Isabella in Angelo's bed: otherwise, she would forever be relegated to solitary uselessness. Shakespeare invests the injured Mariana with a gentle dignity and inwardness that captured the imagination of Victorian readers, yet her eventual plea to marry Angelo, instead of getting even with him when she has the opportunity, implies that a nonreligious woman's only alternative to marriage in Vienna is social death. Although the duke offers to invest her with Angelo's property when he is executed, thus enabling her to "buy" (V.1.423) another husband, her self-respect, along with a perverse, rejected-woman's attachment to him, makes her plead for Angelo's life. She will make do with him.

The polemical charge of Milton's and Marvell's previously cited works, written in the aftermath of a civil war in which the properties of government (I.1.3) had been bloodily disputed on the battlefield, seems absent from Shakespeare's play. Yet both Isabella and Mariana *are* "saved" for marriage through the duke's intervention. Neither Mariana's melancholy self-sufficiency nor Isabella's "fugitive and cloistered virtue" proves tenable in the world of the play. Indeed, the innocence Isabella wishes to maintain becomes subject in the play, and in modern criticism, to interpretations ranging from saintly goodness through simplemindedness to coldness, excessive zeal, seductiveness, and hypocrisy. Far from her own innocence being mirrored by Angelo's, Isabella's innocence tantalizes Angelo and inflames a lust he has never suspected in himself (his own "angelic" innocence thus proves illusory). Whether innocence consists in purity of body and soul from which moral energy flows, or whether it consists in denial, unconsciousness, and even deafness to verbal nuances, is a question constantly posed by the figure of Isabella, both in the play and in subsequent criticism.

"Innocent" and "guilty" meanings are almost inseparably fused in the very language the characters must exchange. When Claudio, for example, asks Lucio to get Isabella to plead for him, he says, "in her youth / There is a prone and speechless dialect, / Such as move men" (I.2.181-83). What this means is that her youthful, feminine helplessness may soften the austere Angelo, yet Isabella's passive sexual body is also already being conceived, however unconsciously, as the "language" most likely to move Angelo. The knowing Lucio, who coaches Isabella, will deliberately exploit her erotic appeal, yet even in her innocence Isabella cannot escape the sexual scenarios embedded in language. When, on her second visit to Angelo, he says, "How now, fair maid!" and she replies, "I am come to know your pleasure" (II.4.30), these perfectly conventional courtesies are innuendo-laden even if neither speaker is conscious of the fact. Innocent intent is not enough to control the effects and implications of the language characters exchange, or to neutralize the erotic charge any statement (or even silence) may take on in a particular context. Any social exchange at all is thus subject to risk. Paradoxically, as Angelo notes, Isabella's innocence operates on him as a more powerful aphrodisiac than would any practiced seductiveness.

Although in different ways, the personal innocence and strict self-government to which Isabella and Angelo aspire crumble in the course of the play. Despite experiencing severe shock and conflict, Angelo succumbs to outright corruption in offering to trade Claudio's life for sex with Isabella. He compounds his guilt by trying to have Claudio executed anyway after Isabella appears to have kept her side of the bargain. Isabella, on the other hand, who retains our respect, becomes party to the somewhat shabby trick in which Mariana is substituted for her in Angelo's bed. Good government, whether public or personal, evidently cannot be predicated on anyone's wholly untarnished innocence.

If this fact becomes clear in the case of Isabella and Angelo, it becomes equally so in the case of the duke. However well-meant his scheme to rectify matters in Vienna, that scheme, which he often seems to be making up as he goes along, depends from the start on deception. He deceives everyone about his intent in leaving the city. In effect, he sets Angelo up for a fall, thus eliciting sympathy for Angelo no matter how badly he behaves. In his disguise as a friar, the duke hoodwinks and manipulates practically everyone. The friar's costume enables him to eavesdrop, hear confessions, and conduct surveillance; even in a good cause, these are the shady arts of political omniscience. His plot to bring about a happy ending not only entails the bed trick but becomes self-serving insofar as he, too, fixes on Isabella, thus making himself Angelo's mirror and rival.

Although there are moments when the duke speaks a language more lofty, oracular, and "inhuman" than that spoken by anyone else in the play, this godlike self-elevation by no means places him above the fray. On the contrary, he seems to regard Lucio's slanders against *him* as more unforgivable than any other crime committed in the play. This personal animus implies that he has been deeply stung by these slanders, the truth or falsity of which we can never fully determine. Yet it is not only the content of the slanders that appears to upset the duke. By going into disguise as a friar, he hears things said about him that he ordinarily would never have heard; such is one risk of assuming a disguise. The duke thus makes the unforeseen discovery that *he,* the ruler, is not immune to gossip and malicious (mis)interpretation. Although he claims that government as such is impaired by irresponsible slander, his vengeful anguish also suggests that he has assumed others see him in the same favorable light as he sees himself. That too is a form of innocence the world will not allow. Even the duke's sexuality, which he denies in his role as friar and presumably wants to keep out of consideration in his exercise of public office, has been a subject of much recent critical speculation, some of it prompted by Lucio's scandalous tales.

If the properties of government are explored in the play, inseparably from the properties of those who govern, so is the condition of the governed, both gentry and commoners. Although Vienna is a class-divided city, a situation that gives rise to both high and low comedy in the play, the sex trade crosses the class divide and seemingly routes all participants to the same destination – namely, the "bath houses" in which mercury vapor is used as a horribly drastic remedy for syphilis. Syphilitic hair loss, disfigurement, and bone decay supply material for countless anxious witticisms in the play, bandied especially among the men-about-town who have good cause to worry. Seeking to ward off the ailment by projecting it onto others seems to be the favored humorous defense mechanism, while calling it "the French disease" implies that it is really foreign to Vienna (or Shakespeare's England). We should recall that syphilis, named by the Italian humanist physician Girolamo Fracastoro in 1530, could still be regarded, mistakenly or otherwise, in Shakespeare's England as a relatively new contagious disease with no safe or reliable cure (the idea of contagion itself being novel). It was certainly seen as representing a threat to the healthy "body politic," and it called into question the age-old medical model under which disease was thought to be caused mainly by humoral imbalances originating inside the body. Like plague before it, and somewhat like AIDS in our own time, epidemic syphilis required that the nature and regulative role of the state be reconsidered. Such forced reflection isn't explicit in *Measure for Measure,* yet syphilis is manifestly one disturbing circumstance to which both governors and governed are reacting in the play.

If sex and death are the great levelers in Vienna (so too is the prison), the sexual marketplace has its own professionals and even mock heroes. The bawd's name Pompey is that of a great Roman general, a fact that produces several jokes at his expense. (Escalus remarks that Pompey's greatness consists, unlike that of his Roman namesake, in the size of his bum, or buttocks, Bum also happening to be this Pompey's vulgar surname.) Modern readers may find it puzzling that the names of legendary Roman generals, Pompey and Caesar, along with that of the Carthaginian leader Hannibal, are rudely bandied about in the Viennese street. A Jacobean debasement of legendary masculine virtue, as well as of the "field" of male action, may be implied by this transposition. We should recall, however, that James I billed himself as a peacemaking king, uniting the kingdom and even trying to outlaw the piracy Englishmen had engaged in with tacit royal sanction during Elizabeth I's reign (the imprisonment of the pirate Ragozine in the play makes the point). Debasement of heroic, warrior masculinity would not necessarily have been inconsistent with James's goals. His own Roman model was the peacemaking, law-giving Augustus Caesar, not the Julius who had ignited the civil wars in Italy. In the play, the mock hero Pompey disturbs the peace and good order of the city. In any event, as an irrepressibly humorous scofflaw and dauntless spokesperson for his trade, Pompey gets short shrift under Angelo's regime; unlike the good-natured, vacillating Escalus,

Angelo does not bandy words with offenders. Nevertheless, it seems unlikely that Angelo's short-lived, self-deconstructing reform will have much lasting effect. It would appear that, in its Jacobean context, the play can end only by staging prospective marriage, however questionably, as good social policy. That outcome is not without irony given James I's own perceived preference for men, a preference the duke in *Measure for Measure* has been suspected by some critics of sharing.

In conclusion, then, why "measure for measure"? For a long time, critics have recognized the allusion of the play's title to Matthew 7:1-2, a passage from Christ's Sermon on the Mount: "Judge not, that ye be not judged. For with what judgment ye judge, ye shall be judged: and with what measure ye mete, it shall be measured to you again." The title phrase, repeated in the play, orients us toward the biblical horizon of much Jacobean thinking on questions of law and morality; it reminds us as well that Shakespeare's culture was deeply infused with biblical lore and citation. To return in conclusion to *Basilikon Doron,* James wrote that "As ye are a good Christian, so may ye be a good king . . . a good king, thinking his highest honor to consist in the due discharge of his calling, employeth all his study and pains to procure and maintain, by the making and execution of good laws, the welfare and peace of his people" (18). With reference to these overlapping religious and political contexts, critics have often debated both the quality of the justice the play delivers and its attempt to balance the respective claims of Law and Mercy. Few critics have argued, however, that the play effectively closes the gap between biblical precept and social implementation. Perhaps it is the difficulty of doing so that *Measure for Measure* highlights above all.

JONATHAN CREWE
Dartmouth College

Note on the Text

MEASURE FOR MEASURE was first printed in the 1623 folio edition of Shakespeare's works. I have followed that text throughout, with only occasional, minor departures. In keeping with this hands-off policy, I have generally adhered to the folio stage directions, even in the few cases where they present problems. There is little about the staging of the play that cannot be left to the initiative of readers and directors. I have, however, followed the scene division of the previous Pelican editor, R. C. Bald, where that division differs from the folio scene division. I have also incorporated much of Bald's editorial work. The punctuation has been modernized, in keeping with standard practice for the new Pelican Shakespeare. Material departures from the folio text are listed below, with the adopted reading in italics followed by the folio reading in roman.

The Names of All the Actors . . . The Scene: Vienna (printed at the end of the play in F)
I.2 12 *Why,* Why? 133 *morality* mortality
I.3 27 *Becomes* (not in F) 43 *it* in
I.4 54 *givings-out* giving-out 78 *make* makes
II.1 12 *your* our 39 *breaks* brakes 67 *honor* – honour. 70 *woman* – woman.
II.2 58 *back* (not in F) 96 *new* now 99 *ere* here 149 *sicles* Sickles
II.4 9 *seared* feard 52 *or* and 75 *me* (not in F) 93 *all-binding* all-building 126 *Women, help heaven!* Women? Helpe heaven;
III.1 29 *sire* fire 52 *me to hear them* them to heare me 68 *Though* Through 90 *enew* emmew 95 *damnedest* damnest 129 *penury* periury 212 *by* to
III.2 23 *array* away 37 *Free from* From 45 *it* (not in F) 71 *bondage; if* bondage if 144 *dearer* deare 214 *and* and as
IV.1 3 *day,* day 25 *welcome* well come 58 **s.d.** *Exeunt* Exit
IV.2 56 *yare* y'are 58 **s.d.** *Exeunt* Exit 99 *lordship's* Lords 141 *reckless* wreaklesse
IV.3 7 *Marry, then* marrie then, 15 *Forthright* Forthlight 22 *What . . .*

Barnardine! (followed in F by s.d. "Barnardine within.")   **88** *yonder* yond   **104** *I'll . . . speed* (followed in F by s.d. "Isabell within.")

IV.4 2 *manner.* manner,   **5** *redeliver* reliver   **13–16** *Well, I . . . you well* (prose in F)   **24** *off* of   **30** *lived* livèd

IV.5 6 *Flavius'* Flavia's

V.1 13 *me* we   **117** *ripened* ripenèd   **169** *her face* your face   **182–83** *Silence . . . himself* (prose in F)   **226** *affianced* affiancèd   **259** *My . . . throughly* (prose in F)   **304** *unhallowed* unhallowèd   **377 s.d.** *Exeunt* Exit   **421** *confiscation* confutation   **444** *governed* governèd   **475 s.d.** *Juliet* Iulietta   **537** *that's* that

Measure for Measure

THE NAMES OF ALL THE ACTORS

VINCENTIO, *the duke*
ANGELO, *the deputy*
ESCALUS, *an ancient lord*
CLAUDIO, *a young gentleman*
LUCIO, *a fantastic*
TWO OTHER LIKE GENTLEMEN
[VARRIUS, *a gentleman attending on the duke*]
PROVOST
[A JUSTICE]
THOMAS ⎱ *two friars*
PETER ⎰
ELBOW, *a simple constable*
FROTH, *a foolish gentleman*
CLOWN *[Pompey]*
ABHORSON, *an executioner*
BARNARDINE, *a dissolute prisoner*
ISABELLA, *sister to Claudio*
MARIANA, *betrothed to Angelo*
JULIET, *beloved of Claudio*
FRANCISCA, *a nun*
MISTRESS OVERDONE, *a bawd*
[LORDS, OFFICERS, CITIZENS, BOY, AND
   ATTENDANTS]

THE SCENE: *Vienna*
*

Measure for Measure

~ **I.1** *Enter Duke, Escalus, Lords [, and Attendants].*

DUKE Escalus.
ESCALUS My lord.
DUKE

Of government the properties to unfold,   3
Would seem in me t' affect speech and discourse,   4
Since I am put to know that your own science   5
Exceeds, in that, the lists of all advice   6
My strength can give you. Then no more remains
But that, to your sufficiency, as your worth is able,   8
And let them work. The nature of our people,
Our city's institutions, and the terms   10
For common justice, you're as pregnant in   11
As art and practice hath enrichèd any
That we remember. There is our commission,
From which we would not have you warp. Call hither,   14
I say, bid come before us Angelo. *[Exit an Attendant.]*
What figure of us think you he will bear?   16
For you must know, we have with special soul   17
Elected him our absence to supply,
Lent him our terror, dressed him with our love,   19

I.1 The palace of Duke Vincentio **3** *properties* attributes **4** *t' affect . . . discourse* to love speech-making **5** *put to know* i.e., do know; *science* knowledge **6** *lists* limits **8–9** *But . . . work* (some words or lines missing?) **10** *terms* legal enactments **11** *pregnant* well-versed **14** *warp* deviate **16** *What . . . bear* i.e., what image of me will he present **17** *with special soul* after deep consideration **19** *terror* awesome power

20   And given his deputation all the organs
      Of our own power. What think you of it?

ESCALUS
      If any in Vienna be of worth
23   To undergo such ample grace and honor,
      It is Lord Angelo.

Enter Angelo.

DUKE   Look where he comes.

ANGELO
      Always obedient to your grace's will,
      I come to know your pleasure.

DUKE   Angelo,
27   There is a kind of character in thy life,
      That to th' observer doth thy history
29   Fully unfold. Thyself and thy belongings
30   Are not thine own so proper, as to waste
      Thyself upon thy virtues, they on thee.
      Heaven doth with us as we with torches do,
      Not light them for themselves; for if our virtues
      Did not go forth of us, 'twere all alike
35   As if we had them not. Spirits are not finely touched
36   But to fine issues, nor nature never lends
37   The smallest scruple of her excellence
38   But like a thrifty goddess she determines
      Herself the glory of a creditor,
40   Both thanks and use. But I do bend my speech
41   To one that can my part in him advertise.
      Hold therefore, Angelo:
43   In our remove be thou at full ourself.
      Mortality and mercy in Vienna

---

20 *deputation* office as deputy; *organs* instruments   **23** *undergo* uphold   **27** *character* readable script   **29** *belongings* attributes   **30** *proper* exclusively   **30–31** *as to waste . . . on thee* i.e., to waste yourself on your own virtues or waste them only on yourself   **35** *finely touched* nobly stirred   **36** *But . . . issues* i.e., unless something fine comes from them   **37** *scruple* minute particle   **38** *determines* awards   **40** *use* interest   **41** *that . . . advertise* i.e., can instruct himself in playing my part   **43** *remove* absence

Live in thy tongue and heart. Old Escalus,
Though first in question, is thy secondary.   46
Take thy commission.

ANGELO   Now, good my lord,
Let there be some more test made of my mettle   48
Before so noble and so great a figure
Be stamped upon it.   50

DUKE   No more evasion.
We have with a leavened and preparèd choice   51
Proceeded to you, therefore take your honors.
Our haste from hence is of so quick condition   53
That it prefers itself, and leaves unquestioned   54
Matters of needful value. We shall write to you,   55
As time and our concernings shall importune,   56
How it goes with us, and do look to know
What doth befall you here. So fare you well:
To th' hopeful execution do I leave you
Of your commissions.   60

ANGELO   Yet give leave, my lord,
That we may bring you something on the way.   61

DUKE
My haste may not admit it.
Nor need you, on mine honor, have to do
With any scruple; your scope is as mine own,   64
So to enforce or qualify the laws   65
As to your soul seems good. Give me your hand.
I'll privily away. I love the people,   67
But do not like to stage me to their eyes.
Though it do well, I do not relish well   69

---

46 *in question* in rank and in my consideration   48 *mettle* worth (punning
on "metal")   50 *stamped* i.e., as on a coin blank   51 *leavened* well-
considered (i.e., yeasted and risen like good bread)   53 *is . . . condition* is so
urgent   54 *prefers* takes precedence; *unquestioned* unconsidered   55 *needful
value* pressing importance   56 *concernings . . . importune* concerns require
61 *something* some distance   64 *scruple* hesitation   65 *qualify* mitigate   67
privily secretly   69 *Though . . . do well* even if it is fitting

70   Their loud applause and aves vehement,
71   Nor do I think the man of safe discretion
72   That does affect it. Once more, fare you well.

ANGELO
      The heavens give safety to your purposes!

ESCALUS
      Lead forth and bring you back in happiness!

DUKE
      I thank you; fare you well.   *Exit.*

ESCALUS
      I shall desire you, sir, to give me leave
      To have free speech with you; and it concerns me
78   To look into the bottom of my place.
      A power I have, but of what strength and nature
80   I am not yet instructed.

ANGELO
      'Tis so with me. Let us withdraw together,
82   And we may soon our satisfaction have
      Touching that point.

ESCALUS   I'll wait upon your honor. *Exeunt.*

                          *

∿ I.2 *Enter Lucio and two other Gentlemen.*

LUCIO   If the duke, with the other dukes, come not to
2   composition with the King of Hungary, why then all
3   the dukes fall upon the king.

FIRST GENTLEMAN   Heaven grant us its peace, but not
5   the King of Hungary's!

SECOND GENTLEMAN   Amen.

_____

70 *aves* salutations   71 *safe discretion* good judgment   72 *affect* like, enjoy
78 *bottom* full extent; *place* power, position   82 *satisfaction* full understanding
    I.2 A street in Vienna   2 *composition* agreement   3 *fall upon* attack, devour
5 *Hungary's* (pun on "hungry")

LUCIO Thou conclud'st like the sanctimonious pirate, that went to sea with the Ten Commandments, but scraped one out of the table. 9

SECOND GENTLEMAN "Thou shalt not steal"? 10

LUCIO Ay, that he razed. 11

FIRST GENTLEMAN Why, 'twas a commandment to command the captain and all the rest from their functions: 13 they put forth to steal. There's not a soldier of us all that, in the thanksgiving before meat, do relish the petition well that prays for peace.

SECOND GENTLEMAN I never heard any soldier dislike it.

LUCIO I believe thee, for I think thou never wast where grace was said.

SECOND GENTLEMAN No? A dozen times at least. 20

FIRST GENTLEMAN What? In meter? 21

LUCIO In any proportion or in any language. 22

FIRST GENTLEMAN I think, or in any religion.

LUCIO Ay, why not? Grace is grace, despite of all contro- 24 versy: as, for example, thou thyself art a wicked villain, despite of all grace.

SECOND GENTLEMAN Well, there went but a pair of 27 shears between us.

LUCIO I grant, as there may between the lists and the 29 velvet. Thou art the list. 30

FIRST GENTLEMAN And thou the velvet. Thou art good 31 velvet; thou'rt a three-piled piece, I warrant thee. I had as lief be a list of an English kersey as be piled, as thou 33 art piled, for a French velvet. Do I speak feelingly now? 34

---

9 *table* tablet   11 *razed* erased   13 *functions* occupations   21 *in meter* i.e., a rhyming grace   22 *proportion* (poetic) form   24–26 *Grace . . . grace* (wordplay on *grace* as divine gift and a prayer before a meal)   27–28 *there went . . . us* i.e., we are cut from the same cloth   29 *lists* the plain edges of fancy velvet cloth   31–34 *Thou . . . velvet* (wordplay on *piled* as the nap of *velvet* and "pilled" as plucked threadbare, the latter in reference to hair loss through syphilis – the "*French* disease")   33 *kersey* plain, homespun cloth   34 *feelingly* eloquently

35 LUCIO   I think thou dost, and indeed with most painful
feeling of thy speech. I will, out of thine own confes-
37 sion, learn to begin thy health, but, whilst I live, forget
to drink after thee.

39 FIRST GENTLEMAN   I think I have done myself wrong,
40 have I not?

SECOND GENTLEMAN   Yes, that thou hast, whether thou
42 art tainted or free.

Enter Bawd [Mistress Overdone].

43 LUCIO   Behold, behold, where Madam Mitigation comes!
I have purchased as many diseases under her roof as
come to –

SECOND GENTLEMAN   To what, I pray?

LUCIO   Judge.

48 SECOND GENTLEMAN   To three thousand dolors a year.

FIRST GENTLEMAN   Ay, and more.

50 LUCIO   A French crown more.

51 FIRST GENTLEMAN   Thou art always figuring diseases in
me, but thou art full of error. I am sound.

LUCIO   Nay, not – as one would say – healthy, but so
54 sound as things that are hollow. Thy bones are hollow;
55 impiety has made a feast of thee.

FIRST GENTLEMAN   How now, which of your hips has the
57 most profound sciatica?

MISTRESS OVERDONE   Well, well. There's one yonder arrested and carried to prison was worth five thousand of
60 you all.

35–36 *painful feeling* i.e., syphilitic sores make speaking painful 37
learn . . . health i.e., like a priest, teach you better   37–38 *forget . . . thee* i.e.,
I'll drink to your health, but not from the same cup (for fear of infection)
39 *done myself wrong* i.e., embarrassingly set myself up for your jibes 42
tainted or free infected or free from infection   43 *Madam Mitigation* (so addressed because as prostitute and brothel keeper she "mitigates" men's desires) 48 *dolors* pains (punning on "dollars") 50 *French crown* (1) gold
coin, (2) bald head caused by syphilis 51 *figuring* imagining 54 *bones . . .
hollow* i.e., consumed by venereal disease 55 *impiety* bad conduct 57 *profound sciatica* i.e., deepest pain

SECOND GENTLEMAN Who's that, I pray thee?

MISTRESS OVERDONE Marry, sir, that's Claudio, Signor Claudio.

FIRST GENTLEMAN Claudio to prison? 'Tis not so.

MISTRESS OVERDONE Nay, but I know 'tis so. I saw him arrested, saw him carried away, and, which is more, within these three days his head to be chopped off.

LUCIO But, after all this fooling, I would not have it so. Art thou sure of this?

MISTRESS OVERDONE I am too sure of it, and it is for get- 70
ting Madam Julietta with child.

LUCIO Believe me, this may be. He promised to meet me two hours since, and he was ever precise in promise- 73
keeping.

SECOND GENTLEMAN Besides, you know, it draws some-thing near to the speech we had to such a purpose.

FIRST GENTLEMAN But most of all, agreeing with the proclamation.

LUCIO Away, let's go learn the truth of it.

       Exit [Lucio with the Gentlemen].

MISTRESS OVERDONE Thus what with the war, what 80
with the sweat, what with the gallows, and what with 81
poverty, I am custom-shrunk. 82

 Enter Clown [Pompey].

How now? What's the news with you?

POMPEY Yonder man is carried to prison.

MISTRESS OVERDONE Well, what has he done?

POMPEY A woman.

MISTRESS OVERDONE But what's his offense?

POMPEY Groping for trouts in a peculiar river. 88

MISTRESS OVERDONE What? Is there a maid with child by him? 90

---

73 *precise* punctilious 81 *sweat* sweating sickness 82 *custom-shrunk* short of customers 88 *Groping . . . river* (alludes, with sexual innuendo, to catch-ing trout by tickling their gills); *peculiar* private, off limits

POMPEY   No, but there's a woman with maid by him.
You have not heard of the proclamation, have you?
MISTRESS OVERDONE   What proclamation, man?
94 POMPEY   All houses in the suburbs of Vienna must be
plucked down.
MISTRESS OVERDONE   And what shall become of those in
the city?
98 POMPEY   They shall stand for seed. They had gone down
99 too, but that a wise burgher put in for them.
100 MISTRESS OVERDONE   But shall all our houses of resort in
the suburbs be pulled down?
POMPEY   To the ground, mistress.
MISTRESS OVERDONE   Why, here's a change indeed in the
commonwealth! What shall become of me?
POMPEY   Come, fear not you; good counselors lack no
clients. Though you change your place, you need not
107 change your trade. I'll be your tapster still. Courage,
there will be pity taken on you; you that have worn
your eyes almost out in the service, you will be consid-
110 ered.
MISTRESS OVERDONE   What's to do here, Thomas Tapster? Let's withdraw.
POMPEY   Here comes Signor Claudio, led by the provost
to prison; and there's Madam Juliet.   *Exeunt.*
*Enter Provost, Claudio, Juliet, Officers, Lucio, and two
Gentlemen.*

CLAUDIO
Fellow, why dost thou show me thus to th' world?
Bear me to prison, where I am committed.

PROVOST
117 I do it not in evil disposition,

---

94 *houses* brothels; *suburbs* areas outside city jurisdiction where brothels and
playhouses were located   98 *stand for seed* be maintained for future propagation   99 *burgher* prosperous citizen   100 *houses of resort* brothels   107 *tapster* barman   117 *evil disposition* malicious nature

But from Lord Angelo by special charge.

CLAUDIO
Thus can the demigod Authority
Make us pay down for our offense by weight.   120
The words of heaven: on whom it will, it will;   121
On whom it will not, so. Yet still 'tis just.

LUCIO
Why, how now, Claudio? Whence comes this restraint?

CLAUDIO
From too much liberty, my Lucio, liberty.
As surfeit is the father of much fast,   125
So every scope by the immoderate use   126
Turns to restraint. Our natures do pursue,
Like rats that ravin down their proper bane,   128
A thirsty evil, and when we drink we die.   129

LUCIO   If I could speak so wisely under an arrest, I would   130
send for certain of my creditors. And yet, to say the
truth, I had as lief have the foppery of freedom as the   132
morality of imprisonment. What's thy offense, Claudio?

CLAUDIO
What but to speak of would offend again.

LUCIO   What, is't murder?

CLAUDIO   No.

LUCIO   Lechery?

CLAUDIO   Call it so.

PROVOST   Away, sir, you must go.   140

CLAUDIO
One word, good friend. Lucio, a word with you.

---

120 *pay . . . weight* i.e., pay the heavy bill (alluding to the number and
weight of coins) 121 *words of heaven* biblical prohibitions on loose living
121–22 *on whom . . . just* i.e., heaven inscrutably punishes whomever it will,
but is *just* nevertheless 125 *surfeit* overindulgence, gluttony 126 *scope*
freedom, opportunity 128 *ravin . . . bane* gorge the poison specifically
compounded for them 129 *thirsty* i.e., both causing and experienced as
thirst 132 *I had as lief* I'd just as soon; *foppery* frivolity

LUCIO   A hundred, if they'll do you any good. Is lechery
143   so looked after?

CLAUDIO

144   Thus stands it with me: upon a true contract
        I got possession of Julietta's bed.
146   You know the lady; she is fast my wife
147   Save that we do the denunciation lack
148   Of outward order. This we came not to
149   Only for propagation of a dower
150   Remaining in the coffer of her friends,
151   From whom we thought it meet to hide our love
        Till time had made them for us. But it chances
153   The stealth of our most mutual entertainment
154   With character too gross is writ on Juliet.

LUCIO
        With child, perhaps?

CLAUDIO   Unhappily, even so.
        And the new deputy now for the duke –
157   Whether it be the fault and glimpse of newness,
        Or whether that the body public be
        A horse whereon the governor doth ride,
160   Who, newly in the seat, that it may know
        He can command, lets it straight feel the spur;
162   Whether the tyranny be in his place,
163   Or in his eminence that fills it up,
164   I stagger in – but this new governor
165   Awakes me all the enrollèd penalties
        Which have, like unscoured armor, hung by th' wall
167   So long that nineteen zodiacs have gone round

---

143 *looked after* actively investigated   144 *true contract* legally binding
promise to marry   146 *fast* securely   147 *denunciation* declaration   148
outward order public ceremony   149 *propagation* begetting (i.e., her dowry
wasn't yet fully made up)   150 *coffer* treasure chest; *friends* family   151 *meet*
appropriate   153 *entertainment* enjoyment   154 *gross* large, plainly legible
157 *glimpse* blinding shimmer   162 *place* position   163 *eminence* self-
importance   164 *I stagger in* I'm unsure   165 *Awakes me* revives in my case;
enrollèd recorded in the rolls of the law   167 *zodiacs* i.e., years

And none of them been worn; and for a name   168
Now puts the drowsy and neglected act
Freshly on me. 'Tis surely for a name.   *170*

LUCIO   I warrant it is, and thy head stands so tickle on   171
thy shoulders that a milkmaid, if she be in love, may
sigh it off. Send after the duke and appeal to him.

CLAUDIO
I have done so, but he's not to be found.
I prithee, Lucio, do me this kind service:
This day my sister should the cloister enter,   176
And there receive her approbation.   177
Acquaint her with the danger of my state;
Implore her, in my voice, that she make friends
To the strict deputy; bid herself assay him.   180
I have great hope in that; for in her youth
There is a prone and speechless dialect,   182
Such as move men; beside, she hath prosperous art   183
When she will play with reason and discourse,   184
And well she can persuade.

LUCIO   I pray she may, as well for the encouragement of
the like, which else would stand under grievous imposi-   187
tion, as for the enjoying of thy life, who I would be
sorry should be thus foolishly lost at a game of ticktack. 189
I'll to her.   *190*

CLAUDIO
I thank you, good friend Lucio.

LUCIO
Within two hours.

CLAUDIO   Come, officer, away.   *Exeunt.*

                              *

---

168 *for a name* i.e., to gain a reputation **171** *tickle* precariously poised
176 *cloister* nunnery **177** *approbation* admission as a novice **180** *assay* as-
sail, try **182** *prone* ready; *dialect* language **183** *prosperous* that which pros-
pers **184** *play with* employ **187** *the like* i.e., transgressions like Claudio's
187–88 *imposition* penalty **189** *ticktack* (game similar to backgammon,
here with sexual innuendo)

∾ **I.3** *Enter Duke and Friar Thomas.*

DUKE

No, holy father, throw away that thought;

2   Believe not that the dribbling dart of love

3   Can pierce a complete bosom. Why I desire thee

4   To give me secret harbor hath a purpose

More grave and wrinkled than the aims and ends

Of burning youth.

FRIAR   May your grace speak of it?

DUKE

My holy sir, none better knows than you

8   How I have ever loved the life removed

9   And held in idle price to haunt assemblies

10   Where youth and cost witless bravery keeps.

I have delivered to Lord Angelo,

12   A man of stricture and firm abstinence,

My absolute power and place here in Vienna,

And he supposes me traveled to Poland;

15   For so I have strewed it in the common ear,

And so it is received. Now, pious sir,

You will demand of me why I do this?

FRIAR

Gladly, my lord.

DUKE

We have strict statutes and most biting laws,

20   The needful bits and curbs to headstrong weeds,

21   Which for this fourteen years we have let slip,

22   Even like an o'ergrown lion in a cave,

23   That goes not out to prey. Now, as fond fathers,

Having bound up the threat'ning twigs of birch,

I.3 A friar's cell   **2** *dribbling . . . love* weak or misdirected arrow of love   **3** *complete* lacking nothing, well-fortified   **4** *harbor* lodging   **8** *removed* retired   **9** *assemblies* large social gatherings   **10** *witless bravery* foolish ostentation   **12** *stricture* strictness   **15** *strewed* spread   **21** *fourteen* (cf. *nineteen* in I.2.167)   **22** *o'ergrown* fat and lazy   **23** *fond* doting

Only to stick it in their children's sight
For terror, not to use, in time the rod
Becomes more mocked than feared. So our decrees,
Dead to infliction, to themselves are dead,   28
And liberty plucks justice by the nose,   29
The baby beats the nurse, and quite athwart   30
Goes all decorum.   31
FRIAR   It rested in your grace
To unloose this tied-up justice when you pleased;
And it in you more dreadful would have seemed   33
Than in Lord Angelo.
DUKE   I do fear, too dreadful.
Sith 'twas my fault to give the people scope,
'Twould be my tyranny to strike and gall them   36
For what I bid them do. For we bid this be done   37
When evil deeds have their permissive pass
And not the punishment. Therefore, indeed, my father,
I have on Angelo imposed the office,   40
Who may, in th' ambush of my name, strike home,   41
And yet my nature never in the fight   42
To do it slander. And to behold his sway   43
I will, as 'twere a brother of your order,
Visit both prince and people. Therefore, I prithee,
Supply me with the habit, and instruct me
How I may formally in person bear   47
Like a true friar. More reasons for this action
At our more leisure shall I render you;
Only this one: Lord Angelo is precise,   50
Stands at a guard with envy, scarce confesses   51

---

28 *Dead to infliction* unenforced   **29** *liberty* license   **30** *athwart* awry   **31** *decorum* good behavior; *rested in* remained in   **33** *dreadful* to be feared and respected   **36** *gall* hurt (from chafing suffered by horses with ill-fitting saddles)   **37–39** *we bid . . . punishment* i.e., in effect, we order people to sin when we permit them to sin without punishment   **41** *ambush* cover   **42–43** *never . . . slander* never exposed to detraction (?)   **43** *sway* rule   **47** *formally . . . bear* i.e., conduct myself properly in bearing and manner   **50** *precise* correct   **51** *Stands . . . envy* is on his guard against malicious detraction

That his blood flows, or that his appetite
Is more to bread than stone. Hence shall we see,
54   If power change purpose, what our seemers be.

                              Exit [with Friar].

                        ✳

∾ **I.4** *Enter Isabella and Francisca, a Nun.*

ISABELLA
    And have you nuns no farther privileges?
NUN
    Are not these large enough?
ISABELLA
    Yes, truly. I speak not as desiring more,
    But rather wishing a more strict restraint
5   Upon the sisterhood, the votarists of Saint Clare.
        Lucio within.
LUCIO
    Ho! Peace be in this place.
ISABELLA   Who's that which calls?
NUN
    It is a man's voice. Gentle Isabella,
    Turn you the key, and know his business of him.
    You may, I may not; you are yet unsworn.
10   When you have vowed, you must not speak with men
    But in the presence of the prioress;
    Then, if you speak, you must not show your face,
    Or, if you show your face, you must not speak.
    He calls again; I pray you, answer him.   *[Exit.]*
ISABELLA
    Peace and prosperity; who is't that calls?
        [Enter Lucio.]

---

54 *seemers* those who keep up appearances
I.4 Within the gate of a nunnery   5 *votarists* those bound by religious
vows; *Saint Clare* (founder of the strict religious order Isabella wishes to join)

LUCIO
   Hail, virgin, if you be, as those cheek roses
   Proclaim you are no less. Can you so stead me   17
   As bring me to the sight of Isabella,
   A novice of this place, and the fair sister
   To her unhappy brother, Claudio?   20

ISABELLA
   Why "her unhappy brother"? Let me ask,
   The rather for I now must make you know
   I am that Isabella, his sister.

LUCIO
   Gentle and fair, your brother kindly greets you.
   Not to be weary with you, he's in prison.   25

ISABELLA
   Woe me, for what?

LUCIO
   For that which, if myself might be his judge,
   He should receive his punishment in thanks.
   He hath got his friend with child.

ISABELLA
   Sir, make me not your story.   30

LUCIO   'Tis true.
   I would not, though 'tis my familiar sin
   With maids to seem the lapwing and to jest,   32
   Tongue far from heart, play with all virgins so.
   I hold you as a thing enskied and sainted,   34
   By your renouncement an immortal spirit,
   And to be talked with in sincerity,
   As with a saint.

ISABELLA
   You do blaspheme the good in mocking me.

LUCIO
   Do not believe it. Fewness and truth, 'tis thus: 39

---

17 *stead me* assist me   20 *unhappy* unfortunate   25 *weary* tedious   30 *your story* the butt of your jokes   32 *lapwing* species of bird known for deception   34 *enskied* raised to the heavens   39 *Fewness and truth* briefly and truly

40   Your brother and his lover have embraced.
      As those that feed grow full, as blossoming time
42   That from the seedness the bare fallow brings
43   To teeming foison, even so her plenteous womb
44   Expresseth his full tilth and husbandry.
      ISABELLA
      Someone with child by him? My cousin Juliet?
      LUCIO
      Is she your cousin?
      ISABELLA
47   Adoptedly, as schoolmaids change their names
48   By vain though apt affection.
      LUCIO   She it is.
      ISABELLA
      O, let him marry her!
      LUCIO   This is the point.
50   The duke is very strangely gone from hence;
51   Bore many gentlemen – myself being one –
      In hand, and hope of action; but we do learn
53   By those that know the very nerves of state,
54   His givings-out were of an infinite distance
      From his true-meant design. Upon his place,
      And with full line of his authority,
      Governs Lord Angelo, a man whose blood
      Is very snow broth; one who never feels
59   The wanton stings and motions of the sense,
60   But doth rebate and blunt his natural edge
      With profits of the mind, study and fast.
62   He – to give fear to use and liberty,
      Which have for long run by the hideous law,
      As mice by lions – hath picked out an act

---

42 *seedness* sowing; *fallow* plowed soil   43 *foison* abundant harvest   44 *tilth
and husbandry* plowing and good cultivation (punning on "husband" and alluding to sexual penetration)   47 *Adoptedly* by adoption   48 *vain . . . apt*
foolish though fitting their condition   51–52 *Bore . . . In hand* deceived
53 *nerves* sinews   54 *givings-out* pronouncements   59 *motions . . . sense* sexual passions   60 *rebate* blunt   62 *use* custom

Under whose heavy sense your brother's life   65
Falls into forfeit. He arrests him on it,
And follows close the rigor of the statute
To make him an example. All hope is gone,
Unless you have the grace by your fair prayer
To soften Angelo. And that's my pith of business   70
'Twixt you and your poor brother.

ISABELLA
Doth he so seek his life?   72

LUCIO   Has censured him
Already and, as I hear, the provost hath   73
A warrant for's execution.

ISABELLA
Alas, what poor ability's in me
To do him good?   76

LUCIO   Assay the power you have.

ISABELLA
My power, alas, I doubt.

LUCIO   Our doubts are traitors
And make us lose the good we oft might win,
By fearing to attempt. Go to Lord Angelo
And let him learn to know, when maidens sue   80
Men give like gods; but when they weep and kneel,
All their petitions are as freely theirs   82
As they themselves would owe them.   83

ISABELLA
I'll see what I can do.

LUCIO   But speedily.

ISABELLA
I will about it straight,
No longer staying but to give the mother   86
Notice of my affair. I humbly thank you;

---

65 *heavy sense* weighty application 70 *pith* essence 72 *seek his life* aim to
execute him; *censured* judged 73 *provost* officer charged with the punishment of offenders 76 *Assay* put to the test 80 *sue* plead 82 *petitions* re-
quests 83 *As . . . them* i.e., as if they had entirely gotten their own way; *owe*
possess 86 *mother* mother superior

Commend me to my brother; soon at night
89   I'll send him certain word of my success.
LUCIO
90   I take my leave of you.
ISABELLA   Good sir, adieu.   *Exeunt.*

                              *

∾ **II.1** *Enter Angelo, Escalus, and Servants, Justice.*

ANGELO
       We must not make a scarecrow of the law,
2   Setting it up to fear the birds of prey,
       And let it keep one shape, till custom make it
       Their perch and not their terror.
ESCALUS   Ay, but yet
5   Let us be keen and rather cut a little,
6   Than fall and bruise to death. Alas, this gentleman
       Whom I would save had a most noble father.
       Let but your honor know,
9   Whom I believe to be most strait in virtue,
10   That, in the working of your own affections,
       Had time cohered with place or place with wishing,
12   Or that the resolute acting of your blood
       Could have attained th' effect of your own purpose,
14   Whether you had not sometime in your life
       Erred in this point which now you censure him,
       And pulled the law upon you.
ANGELO
       'Tis one thing to be tempted, Escalus,
       Another thing to fall. I not deny,
19   The jury passing on the prisoner's life
20   May in the sworn twelve have a thief or two

----

89 *my success* i.e., how I fared
    II.1 A courtroom 2 *fear* frighten 5 *keen* sharp 6 *fall* let fall 9 *strait*
strict, upright 10 *affections* passions 12 *resolute . . . blood* i.e., acting with
resolve on the promptings of your desire 14 *had not* would not have 19
passing delivering a verdict

Guiltier than him they try. What's open made to justice,   21
That justice seizes; what knows the laws
That thieves do pass on thieves? 'Tis very pregnant   23
The jewel that we find, we stoop and take't
Because we see it; but what we do not see
We tread upon, and never think of it.
You may not so extenuate his offense
For I have had such faults, but rather tell me,
When I that censure him do so offend,
Let mine own judgment pattern out my death   30
And nothing come in partial. Sir, he must die.   31
     Enter Provost.

ESCALUS
Be it as your wisdom will.
ANGELO   Where is the provost?
PROVOST
Here, if it like your honor.   33
ANGELO   See that Claudio
Be executed by nine tomorrow morning.
Bring him his confessor, let him be prepared,
For that's the utmost of his pilgrimage.   *[Exit Provost.]*   36
ESCALUS
Well, heaven forgive him, and forgive us all.
Some rise by sin, and some by virtue fall;
Some run from breaks of ice, and answer none,   39
And some condemnèd for a fault alone.   40
     Enter Elbow, Froth, Clown [Pompey], Officers.
ELBOW   Come, bring them away. If these be good people
in a commonweal that do nothing but use their abuses   42
in common houses, I know no law. Bring them away.   43

21–23 *What's . . . thieves* i.e., how can the law know when thieves pass judgment on thieves   23 *'Tis . . . pregnant* it makes sense   30 *pattern out* set the example for   31 *come in partial* interfere to bias the outcome   33 *like* please   36 *utmost . . . pilgrimage* end of his life   39 *breaks of ice* (obscure); *answer none* do not have to account for their sins   42 *use their abuses* practice their wrongdoing   43 *common houses* brothels

ANGELO   How now, sir, what's your name? And what's
the matter?

ELBOW   If it please your honor, I am the poor duke's constable, and my name is Elbow. I do lean upon justice,
sir, and do bring in here before your good honor two
notorious benefactors.

50   ANGELO   Benefactors? Well, what benefactors are they?
Are they not malefactors?

ELBOW   If it please your honor, I know not well what
53   they are; but precise villains they are, that I am sure of,
54   and void of all profanation in the world that good
Christians ought to have.

56   ESCALUS   This comes off well; here's a wise officer.

57   ANGELO   Go to. What quality are they of? Elbow is your
name? Why dost thou not speak, Elbow?

59   POMPEY   He cannot, sir; he's out at elbow.

60   ANGELO   What are you, sir?

61   ELBOW   He, sir, a tapster, sir, parcel bawd; one that serves
a bad woman, whose house, sir, was, as they say,
plucked down in the suburbs, and now she professes a
64   hothouse, which I think is a very ill house too.

ESCALUS   How know you that?

ELBOW   My wife, sir, whom I detest before heaven and
your honor –

ESCALUS   How? Thy wife?

ELBOW   Ay, sir, whom I thank heaven is an honest
70   woman –

ESCALUS   Dost thou detest her therefore?

ELBOW   I say, sir, I will detest myself also, as well as she,
73   that this house, if it be not a bawd's house, it is pity of
her life, for it is a naughty house.

---

53 *precise* i.e., "precious," one of Elbow's many malapropisms   54 *profanation* profanity (which Christians ought *not* to have)   56 *comes off well* sounds
good   57 *quality* social status   59 *out at elbow* threadbare (i.e., devoid of
speech)   61 *parcel bawd* partly a bawd   64 *hothouse* bath house   73–74
pity . . . life i.e., it is too bad

ESCALUS   How dost thou know that, constable?

ELBOW   Marry, sir, by my wife, who, if she had been a
woman cardinally given, might have been accused in   77
fornication, adultery, and all uncleanliness there.

ESCALUS   By the woman's means?   79

ELBOW   Ay, sir, by Mistress Overdone's means; but as she   80
spit in his face, so she defied him.

POMPEY   Sir, if it please your honor, this is not so.

ELBOW   Prove it before these varlets here, thou honorable
man, prove it.

ESCALUS   Do you hear how he misplaces?   85

POMPEY   Sir, she came in great with child, and longing –
saving your honor's reverence – for stewed prunes. Sir,   87
we had but two in the house, which at that very distant
time stood, as it were, in a fruit dish, a dish of some
threepence; your honors have seen such dishes; they are   90
not china dishes, but very good dishes –

ESCALUS   Go to, go to; no matter for the dish, sir.

POMPEY   No, indeed, sir, not of a pin, you are therein in
the right: but to the point. As I say, this Mistress Elbow,
being, as I say, with child, and being great-bellied, and
longing, as I said, for prunes, and having but two in the
dish, as I said, Master Froth here, this very man, having
eaten the rest, as I said, and, as I say, paying for them
very honestly, for, as you know, Master Froth, I could
not give you threepence again –   100

FROTH   No, indeed.

POMPEY   Very well! You being then, if you be remem-
bered, cracking the stones of the foresaid prunes –

FROTH   Ay, so I did, indeed.

POMPEY   Why, very well! I telling you then, if you be re-
membered, that such a one and such a one were past

---

77 *cardinally* (he means "carnally")   79 *By . . . means* i.e., at Overdone's in-
stigation   85 *misplaces* transposes words   87 *stewed prunes* (dish associated
with brothels or "stews," with possible obscene reference to testicles)

107   cure of the thing you wot of, unless they kept very good
diet, as I told you –

FROTH   All this is true.

110 POMPEY Why, very well then –

ESCALUS   Come, you are a tedious fool; to the purpose.
What was done to Elbow's wife, that he hath cause to

113   complain of? Come me to what was done to her.

POMPEY   Sir, your honor cannot come to that yet.

ESCALUS   No, sir, nor I mean it not.

POMPEY   Sir, but you shall come to it, by your honor's
leave. And I beseech you look into Master Froth here,
sir, a man of fourscore pound a year, whose father died

119   at Hallowmas. Was't not at Hallowmas, Master Froth?

120 FROTH   Allhallond Eve.

POMPEY Why, very well; I hope here be truths. He, sir,

122   sitting, as I say, in a lower chair, sir – 'twas in the Bunch
of Grapes, where indeed you have a delight to sit, have
you not?

FROTH   I have so, because it is an open room and good
for winter.

POMPEY Why, very well then; I hope here be truths.

ANGELO

    This will last out a night in Russia

    When nights are longest there. I'll take my leave,

130   And leave you to the hearing of the cause,

    Hoping you'll find good cause to whip them all.

ESCALUS

132   I think no less. Good morrow to your lordship.

                                 Exit [Angelo].

    Now, sir, come on; what was done to Elbow's wife,
once more?

POMPEY   Once, sir? There was nothing done to her once.

---

107 *thing you wot of* i.e., syphilis (?) **107–8** *good diet* healthy regimen **113** *Come me to* bring me to **119** *Hallowmas* All Saints' Day (November 1) **120** *Allhallond Eve* (Halloween, October 31: the evening before All Saints' Day) **122** *lower chair* easy chair (?) **122–23** *Bunch of Grapes* (a room at the inn) **130** *cause* case **132** *I . . . less* i.e., very likely

ELBOW   I beseech you, sir, ask him what this man did to
my wife.

POMPEY   I beseech your honor, ask me.

ESCALUS   Well, sir, what did this gentleman to her?

POMPEY   I beseech you, sir, look in this gentleman's face.   *140*
Good Master Froth, look upon his honor; 'tis for a
good purpose. Doth your honor mark his face?

ESCALUS   Ay, sir, very well.

POMPEY   Nay, I beseech you, mark it well.

ESCALUS   Well, I do so.

POMPEY   Doth your honor see any harm in his face?

ESCALUS   Why, no.

POMPEY   I'll be supposed upon a book, his face is the   *148*
worst thing about him. Good, then, if his face be the
worst thing about him, how could Master Froth do   *150*
the constable's wife any harm? I would know that of
your honor.

ESCALUS   He's in the right. Constable, what say you to it?

ELBOW   First, an it like you, the house is a respected   *154*
house; next, this is a respected fellow; and his mistress
is a respected woman.

POMPEY   By this hand, sir, his wife is a more respected
person than any of us all.

ELBOW   Varlet, thou liest; thou liest, wicked varlet. The   *159*
time is yet to come that she was ever respected with   *160*
man, woman, or child.

POMPEY   Sir, she was respected with him before he married with her.

ESCALUS   Which is the wiser here, justice or iniquity? Is
this true?

ELBOW   O thou caitiff, O thou varlet, O thou wicked   *166*
Hannibal! I respected with her before I was married to   *167*
her? If ever I was respected with her, or she with me, let

---

148 *supposed* i.e., deposed **154** *respected* i.e., suspected **159** *Varlet*
scoundrel **166** *caitiff* wretch **167** *Hannibal* Carthaginian general, enemy
of Rome (here confused with "cannibal")

not your worship think me the poor duke's officer.
170 Prove this, thou wicked Hannibal, or I'll have mine ac-
171 tion of batt'ry on thee.

ESCALUS If he took you a box o' th' ear, you might have
your action of slander, too.

ELBOW Marry, I thank your good worship for it. What
is't your worship's pleasure I shall do with this wicked
caitiff?

ESCALUS Truly, officer, because he hath some offenses in
178 him that thou wouldst discover if thou couldst, let him
continue in his courses till thou know'st what they are.

180 ELBOW Marry, I thank your worship for it. Thou seest,
thou wicked varlet, now, what's come upon thee. Thou
art to continue now, thou varlet, thou art to continue.

ESCALUS Where were you born, friend?

FROTH Here in Vienna, sir.

185 ESCALUS Are you of fourscore pounds a year?

FROTH Yes, an't please you, sir.

ESCALUS So. *[To Pompey]* What trade are you of, sir?

POMPEY A tapster, a poor widow's tapster.

ESCALUS Your mistress' name?

190 POMPEY Mistress Overdone.

ESCALUS Hath she had any more than one husband?

POMPEY Nine, sir; Overdone by the last.

ESCALUS Nine! Come hither to me, Master Froth. Master Froth, I would not have you acquainted with tap-
195 sters; they will draw you, Master Froth, and you will
196 hang them. Get you gone, and let me hear no more of
you.

FROTH I thank your worship. For mine own part, I
never come into any room in a taphouse but I am
200 drawn in.

ESCALUS Well, no more of it, Master Froth; farewell.
[Exit Froth.]

---

171 *batt'ry* assault 178 *discover* expose 185 *of* worth 195 *draw you* (1)
entice, (2) drain, (3) gut 196 *hang them* cause them to be hanged

Come you hither to me, master tapster. What's your
name, master tapster?

POMPEY Pompey.

ESCALUS What else?

POMPEY Bum, sir.

ESCALUS Troth, and your bum is the greatest thing
about you, so that, in the beastliest sense, you are Pom- 208
pey the Great. Pompey, you are partly a bawd, Pompey,
howsoever you color it in being a tapster, are you not? 210
Come, tell me true; it shall be the better for you.

POMPEY Truly, sir, I am a poor fellow that would live.

ESCALUS How would you live, Pompey? By being a
bawd? What do you think of the trade, Pompey? Is it a
lawful trade?

POMPEY If the law would allow it, sir.

ESCALUS But the law will not allow it, Pompey, nor it
shall not be allowed in Vienna.

POMPEY Does your worship mean to geld and splay all 219
the youth of the city? 220

ESCALUS No, Pompey.

POMPEY Truly, sir, in my poor opinion, they will to't
then. If your worship will take order for the drabs and 223
the knaves, you need not to fear the bawds.

ESCALUS There is pretty orders beginning, I can tell you;
it is but heading and hanging. 226

POMPEY If you head and hang all that offend that way
but for ten year together, you'll be glad to give out a 228
commission for more heads. If this law hold in Vienna
ten year, I'll rent the fairest house in it after threepence 230
a bay; if you live to see this come to pass, say Pompey 231
told you so.

208–9 *Pompey the Great* a famous Roman general, rival of Julius Caesar
210 *color* disguise   **219** *geld and splay* castrate, neuter   **223** *drabs* prostitutes
226 *heading* beheading   **228–29** *give . . . commission* issue an order   **231**
bay part of a house under a gable

233 ESCALUS Thank you, good Pompey, and, in requital of
your prophecy, hark you. I advise you, let me not find
you before me again upon any complaint whatsoever;
no, not for dwelling where you do. If I do, Pompey, I
237 shall beat you to your tent and prove a shrewd Caesar
to you. In plain dealing, Pompey, I shall have you
whipped. So, for this time, Pompey, fare you well.

240 POMPEY I thank your worship for your good counsel;
[Aside] but I shall follow it as the flesh and fortune shall
better determine.

243 Whip me! No, no, let carman whip his jade;
The valiant heart's not whipped out of his trade. *Exit.*

ESCALUS Come hither to me, Master Elbow; come
hither, master constable. How long have you been in
this place of constable?

ELBOW Seven year and a half, sir.

ESCALUS I thought, by the readiness in the office, you
250 had continued in it some time. You say, seven years together?

ELBOW And a half, sir.

ESCALUS Alas, it hath been great pains to you; they do
254 you wrong to put you so oft upon't. Are there not men
255 in your ward sufficient to serve it?

ELBOW Faith, sir, few of any wit in such matters. As they
257 are chosen, they are glad to choose me for them. I do it
for some piece of money, and go through with all.

ESCALUS Look you bring me in the names of some six or
260 seven, the most sufficient of your parish.

ELBOW To your worship's house, sir?

ESCALUS To my house. Fare you well.   *[Exit Elbow.]*
What's o'clock, think you?

JUSTICE Eleven, sir.

ESCALUS I pray you home to dinner with me.

---

233 *requital* recompense **237–38** *beat . . . to you* (when his army was
routed by Julius Caesar's in 48 BCE, Pompey retired to his tent) **243** *carman*
carter; *jade* worn-out horse **254** *put . . . upon't* impose it on you so often
255 *ward* city district **257** *for them* in their place **260** *sufficient* substantial

JUSTICE   I humbly thank you.

ESCALUS
   It grieves me for the death of Claudio,
   But there's no remedy.

JUSTICE
   Lord Angelo is severe.

ESCALUS   It is but needful.
   Mercy is not itself, that oft looks so;   *270*
   Pardon is still the nurse of second woe.
   But yet poor Claudio; there is no remedy.
   Come, sir.   *Exeunt.*

*

∽ **II.2** *Enter Provost, [and a] Servant.*

SERVANT
   He's hearing of a cause; he will come straight.
   I'll tell him of you.

PROVOST   Pray you, do. *[Exit Servant.]* I'll
   know
   His pleasure; may be he will relent. Alas,
   He hath but as offended in a dream.   4
   All sects, all ages smack of this vice – and he   5
   To die for't!
      Enter Angelo.

ANGELO   Now, what's the matter, provost?

PROVOST
   Is it your will Claudio shall die tomorrow?

ANGELO
   Did not I tell thee, yea? Hadst thou not order?
   Why dost thou ask again?

PROVOST   Lest I might be too rash.
   Under your good correction, I have seen   10

II.2 In Angelo's house   **4** *He . . . dream* i.e., both Claudio's state of mind
and the facts make this crime unreal (?)   **5** *sects* kinds of people   **10** *Under*
subject to

When, after execution, judgment hath
12   Repented o'er his doom.

ANGELO   Go to, let that be mine.
Do you your office, or give up your place,
And you shall well be spared.

PROVOST   I crave your honor's
    pardon.
15   What shall be done, sir, with the groaning Juliet?
She's very near her hour.

ANGELO   Dispose of her
To some more fitter place, and that with speed.
    [Enter Servant.]

SERVANT
Here is the sister of the man condemned
Desires access to you.

ANGELO   Hath he a sister?

PROVOST
20   Ay, my good lord, a very virtuous maid,
And to be shortly of a sisterhood,
If not already.

ANGELO   Well, let her be admitted. *[Exit Servant.]*
See you the fornicatress be removed;
Let her have needful, but not lavish, means;
25   There shall be order for't.
    Enter Lucio and Isabella.

PROVOST   'Save your honor.

ANGELO
Stay a little while.
    [To Isabella]   You're welcome. What's your will?

ISABELLA
I am a woeful suitor to your honor,
Please but your honor hear me.

ANGELO   Well, what's your suit?

ISABELLA
There is a vice that most I do abhor,

---

12 *doom* sentence   15 *groaning* i.e., in labor   25 *order* a requisition

And most desire should meet the blow of justice,   *30*
For which I would not plead, but that I must,
For which I must not plead, but that I am
At war 'twixt will and will not.

ANGELO   Well, the matter?

ISABELLA
I have a brother is condemned to die.
I do beseech you, let it be his fault,   *35*
And not my brother.

PROVOST   *[Aside]*   Heaven give thee moving graces.

ANGELO
Condemn the fault, and not the actor of it?
Why, every fault's condemned ere it be done.
Mine were the very cipher of a function,   *39*
To fine the faults whose fine stands in record,   *40*
And let go by the actor.

ISABELLA   O just, but severe law!
I had a brother then. Heaven keep your honor.

LUCIO   *[Aside to Isabella]*
Give't not o'er so. To him again, entreat him,
Kneel down before him, hang upon his gown.
You are too cold. If you should need a pin,
You could not with more tame a tongue desire it.
To him, I say.

ISABELLA
Must he needs die?

ANGELO   Maiden, no remedy.

ISABELLA
Yes, I do think that you might pardon him,
And neither heaven nor man grieve at the mercy.   *50*

ANGELO
I will not do't.

ISABELLA   But can you if you would?

---

35 *let . . . fault* let his fault be condemned   **39** *cipher of a function* meaning-
less official role   **40** *faults . . . record* the faults already condemned by law

ANGELO
52   Look what I will not, that I cannot do.

ISABELLA
        But might you do't, and do the world no wrong,
54   If so your heart were touched with that remorse
        As mine is to him?

ANGELO
        He's sentenced; 'tis too late.

LUCIO   *[Aside to Isabella]*   You are too cold.

ISABELLA
        Too late? Why, no. I that do speak a word
        May call it back again. Well believe this,
59   No ceremony that to great ones 'longs,
60   Not the king's crown, nor the deputed sword,
        The marshal's truncheon, nor the judge's robe,
        Become them with one half so good a grace
        As mercy does.
        If he had been as you, and you as he,
        You would have slipped like him; but he, like you,
        Would not have been so stern.

ANGELO   Pray you, be gone.

ISABELLA
67   I would to heaven I had your potency,
        And you were Isabel; should it then be thus?
69   No, I would tell what 'twere to be a judge,
70   And what a prisoner.

LUCIO   *[Aside to Isabella]*
                                    Ay, touch him; there's the vein.

ANGELO
        Your brother is a forfeit of the law,
        And you but waste your words.

ISABELLA   Alas, alas;

---

52 *Look what* whatever   54 *remorse* pity   59 *'longs* belongs   60 *deputed sword* emblematic sword of power or justice borne by the one *deputed* to wield it   67 *potency* power   69 *tell* proclaim

Why, all the souls that were were forfeit once,   73
And he that might the vantage best have took,   74
Found out the remedy. How would you be,
If he, which is the top of judgment, should   76
But judge you as you are? O think on that,
And mercy then will breathe within your lips,
Like man new made.   79
ANGELO   Be you content, fair maid,
    It is the law, not I, condemn your brother.   80
    Were he my kinsman, brother, or my son,   81
    It should be thus with him. He must die tomorrow.

ISABELLA
    Tomorrow? O, that's sudden; spare him, spare him!
    He's not prepared for death. Even for our kitchens
    We kill the fowl of season; shall we serve heaven   85
    With less respect than we do minister
    To our gross selves? Good, good my lord, bethink you.
    Who is it that hath died for this offense?
    There's many have committed it.

LUCIO   *[Aside to Isabella]*   Ay, well said.

ANGELO
    The law hath not been dead, though it hath slept.   90
    Those many had not dared to do that evil
    If the first that did th' edict infringe
    Had answered for his deed. Now 'tis awake,
    Takes note of what is done, and like a prophet
    Looks in a glass that shows what future evils,   95
    Either new, or by remissness new-conceived,   96
    And so in progress to be hatched and born,   97
    Are now to have no successive degrees,   98
    But, ere they live, to end.

ISABELLA   Yet show some pity.

---

73 *forfeit* lost, doomed   74 *vantage* opportunity   76 *which . . . judgment*
who is the supreme judge   79 *new made* saved, reborn   81 *kinsman* relative
85 *of season* in season   95 *glass* mirror   96 *by remissness* through (our) laxity
97 *in progress* in due course   98 *degrees* stages

ANGELO

100   I show it most of all when I show justice,
       For then I pity those I do not know,
102   Which a dismissed offense would after gall,
103   And do him right that, answering one foul wrong,
       Lives not to act another. Be satisfied;
       Your brother dies tomorrow; be content.

ISABELLA

       So you must be the first that gives this sentence,
       And he, that suffers. O, it is excellent
       To have a giant's strength, but it is tyrannous
       To use it like a giant.

LUCIO   *[Aside to Isabella]*
                              That's well said.

ISABELLA

110   Could great men thunder
       As Jove himself does, Jove would never be quiet,
112   For every pelting, petty officer
       Would use his heaven for thunder,
       Nothing but thunder. Merciful heaven,
       Thou rather with thy sharp and sulphurous bolt
116   Splits the unwedgeable and gnarlèd oak
       Than the soft myrtle; but man, proud man,
       Dressed in a little brief authority,
119   Most ignorant of what he's most assured –
120   His glassy essence – like an angry ape
       Plays such fantastic tricks before high heaven
122   As makes the angels weep; who, with our spleens,
123   Would all themselves laugh mortal.

LUCIO   *[Aside to Isabella]*
       O, to him, to him, wench; he will relent.

---

102 *dismissed* unpunished; *gall* hurt   **103** *do him right* serve him well   **112** *pelting* paltry   **116** *unwedgeable* unsplittable   **119** *assured* confident   **120** *His . . . essence* his own fragile being (?)   **122** *spleen* (believed to be the organ of laughter)   **123** *laugh mortal* laugh themselves to death (into human mortality)

He's coming, I perceive't.

PROVOST   *[Aside]*   Pray heaven she win him.

ISABELLA
We cannot weigh our brother with ourself.   126
Great men may jest with saints, 'tis wit in them,   127
But in the less foul profanation.

LUCIO   *[Aside to Isabella]*
Thou'rt i' th' right, girl, more o' that.

ISABELLA
That in the captain's but a choleric word,   130
Which in the soldier is flat blasphemy.

LUCIO   *[Aside to Isabella]*
Art avised o' that? More on't.   132

ANGELO
Why do you put these sayings upon me?   133

ISABELLA
Because authority, though it err like others,
Hath yet a kind of medicine in itself
That skins the vice o' th' top. Go to your bosom,   136
Knock there, and ask your heart what it doth know
That's like my brother's fault. If it confess
A natural guiltiness such as is his,
Let it not sound a thought upon your tongue   *140*
Against my brother's life.

ANGELO   *[Aside]*   She speaks, and 'tis
Such sense that my sense breeds with it. Fare you well.   142

ISABELLA
Gentle my lord, turn back.

ANGELO
I will bethink me. Come again tomorrow.

ISABELLA
Hark how I'll bribe you; good my lord, turn back.

---

126 *our brother* i.e., our fellow man   **127** *jest with saints* joke about holy persons or subjects; *wit* cleverness   **130** *That* that which; *choleric* angry   **132** *avised* informed   **133** *put* thrust   **136** *skins . . . top* covers over the corruption   **142** *sense that . . . breeds* i.e., her good sense excites my sensuality

ANGELO
How! Bribe me?

ISABELLA
Ay, with such gifts that heaven shall share with you.

LUCIO   *[Aside to Isabella]*
You had marred all else.

ISABELLA
149 Not with fond sicles of the tested gold,
150 Or stones whose rate are either rich or poor
151 As fancy values them, but with true prayers
That shall be up at heaven and enter there
153 Ere sunrise; prayers from preservèd souls,
From fasting maids whose minds are dedicate
To nothing temporal.

ANGELO   Well, come to me tomorrow.

LUCIO   *[Aside to Isabella]*
Go to, 'tis well; away.

ISABELLA
Heaven keep your honor safe.

ANGELO   *[Aside]*   Amen.
For I am that way going to temptation,
159 Where prayers cross.

ISABELLA   At what hour tomorrow
160 Shall I attend your lordship?

ANGELO   At any time 'fore noon.

ISABELLA
'Save your honor. *[Exeunt Isabella, Lucio, and Provost.]*

ANGELO   From thee, even from thy virtue!
What's this? What's this? Is this her fault or mine?
The tempter or the tempted, who sins most, ha?
Not she, nor doth she tempt; but it is I
That, lying by the violet in the sun,
Do as the carrion does, not as the flower,

---

149 *fond sicles* foolish shekels (Jewish currency)   150 *rate are* worth is   151 *fancy* capricious imagination   153 *preservèd* shielded from vice   159 *cross* are at cross purposes

Corrupt with virtuous season. Can it be   167
That modesty may more betray our sense   168
Than woman's lightness? Having waste ground enough,   169
Shall we desire to raze the sanctuary   170
And pitch our evils there? O fie, fie, fie!   171
What dost thou, or what are thou, Angelo?
Dost thou desire her foully for those things
That make her good? O, let her brother live!
Thieves for their robbery have authority
When judges steal themselves. What, do I love her,
That I desire to hear her speak again,
And feast upon her eyes? What is't I dream on?
O cunning enemy that, to catch a saint,   179
With saints dost bait thy hook! Most dangerous   *180*
Is that temptation that doth goad us on
To sin in loving virtue. Never could the strumpet   182
With all her double vigor, art and nature,
Once stir my temper, but this virtuous maid   184
Subdues me quite. Ever till now,
When men were fond, I smiled and wondered how.   186

                                              Exit.

                        *

∾ **II.3** *Enter Duke [disguised as a friar] and Provost.*

DUKE
Hail to you, provost – so I think you are.
PROVOST
I am the provost. What's your will, good friar?
DUKE
Bound by my charity and my blessed order,

---

167 *Corrupt . . . season* rot instead of blooming in the time of growth   **168**
betray . . . sense uncover our sensuality   **169** *lightness* lewdness   **170** *raze the
sanctuary* demolish the holy place of refuge   **171** *pitch our evils* erect our foul
structures (?)   **179** *enemy* Satan   **182** *strumpet* whore   **184** *temper* temper-
ate self-possession   **186** *fond* infatuated
    II.3 A prison

I come to visit the afflicted spirits
Here in the prison. Do me the common right
To let me see them and to make me know
The nature of their crimes, that I may minister
To them accordingly.

PROVOST
I would do more than that, if more were needful.
        Enter Juliet.

10   Look, here comes one, a gentlewoman of mine,
11   Who, falling in the flaws of her own youth,
12   Hath blistered her report. She is with child,
     And he that got it, sentenced, a young man
     More fit to do another such offense
     Than die for this.

DUKE
When must he die?

PROVOST   As I do think, tomorrow.
        [To Juliet]
     I have provided for you; stay a while
     And you shall be conducted.

DUKE
Repent you, fair one, of the sin you carry?

JULIET
20   I do, and bear the shame most patiently.

DUKE
21   I'll teach you how you shall arraign your conscience
     And try your penitence, if it be sound,
23   Or hollowly put on.

JULIET   I'll gladly learn.

DUKE
Love you the man that wronged you?

JULIET
Yes, as I love the woman that wronged him.

---

11 *flaws* gusts of passion 12 *blistered . . . report* damaged her reputation
21 *arraign* charge, accuse 23 *hollowly* falsely

DUKE
  So then it seems your most offenseful act
  Was mutually committed?
JULIET   Mutually.
DUKE
  Then was your sin of heavier kind than his.
JULIET
  I do confess it, and repent it, father.
DUKE
  'Tis meet so, daughter, but lest you do repent   30
  As that the sin hath brought you to this shame,   31
  Which sorrow is always toward ourselves, not heaven,
  Showing we would not spare heaven as we love it,   33
  But as we stand in fear –
JULIET
  I do repent me as it is an evil,
  And take the shame with joy.   36
DUKE   There rest.
  Your partner, as I hear, must die tomorrow,
  And I am going with instruction to him.   38
  Grace go with you. Benedicite.   *Exit.*   39
JULIET
  Must die tomorrow! O injurious love,   40
  That respites me a life whose very comfort
  Is still a dying horror.
PROVOST   'Tis pity of him.   *Exeunt.*
                            *

∾ II.4 *Enter Angelo.*

ANGELO
  When I would pray and think, I think and pray

_____
30 *meet* fitting **31** *As that* because **33** *spare* i.e., refrain from offending
36 *There rest* don't change your view **38** *instruction* religious counsel **39**
Benedicite bless you
  II.4 In Angelo's house

2   To several subjects. Heaven hath my empty words,
3   Whilst my invention, hearing not my tongue,
       Anchors on Isabel. Heaven in my mouth,
       As if I did but only chew his name,
       And in my heart the strong and swelling evil
7   Of my conception. The state, whereon I studied,
       Is like a good thing, being often read,
       Grown seared and tedious; yea, my gravity,
10   Wherein, let no man hear me, I take pride,
11   Could I, with boot, change for an idle plume
12   Which the air beats for vain. O place, O form,
13   How often dost thou with thy case, thy habit,
       Wrench awe from fools, and tie the wiser souls
       To thy false seeming! Blood, thou art blood.
16   Let's write "good Angel" on the devil's horn,
17   'Tis not the devil's crest. How now, who's there?
            Enter Servant.

SERVANT
       One Isabel, a sister, desires access to you.

ANGELO
       Teach her the way. *[Exit Servant.]* O heavens,
20   Why does my blood thus muster to my heart,
21   Making both it unable for itself,
22   And dispossessing all my other parts
       Of necessary fitness?
       So play the foolish throngs with one that swoons,
       Come all to help him, and so stop the air
       By which he should revive; and even so
27   The general, subject to a well-wished king,

---

2 *several* separate   3 *invention* imagination   7 *conception* thought; *state*
statecraft   11 *with boot* profitably; *plume* showy feather   12 *for vain* in vain;
place high position; *form* ceremony   13 *case* outward covering; *habit* robes
16 *Angel* (punning on "Angelo")   17 *crest* badge, emblem   21 *unable for itself* unable to perform its tasks   22–23 *And . . . fitness* i.e., depriving the rest
of the body of what it needs   27 *general* populace; *well-wished king* king who
has the people's good wishes

Quit their own part, and in obsequious fondness   28
Crowd to his presence, where their untaught love
Must needs appear offense.   30
    Enter Isabella.

                      How now, fair maid!

ISABELLA
I am come to know your pleasure.

ANGELO
That you might know it would much better please me
Than to demand what 'tis. Your brother cannot live.

ISABELLA
Even so. Heaven keep your honor.

ANGELO
Yet may he live a while, and it may be
As long as you or I; yet he must die.

ISABELLA
Under your sentence?

ANGELO   Yea.

ISABELLA
When, I beseech you? That in his reprieve,   38
Longer or shorter, he may be so fitted   39
That his soul sicken not.   40

ANGELO
Ha! Fie, these filthy vices! It were as good
To pardon him that hath from nature stol'n
A man already made, as to remit   43
Their saucy sweetness that do coin heaven's image   44
In stamps that are forbid. 'Tis all as easy
Falsely to take away a life true made,
As to put mettle in restrainèd means   47
To make a false one.

---

28 *part* places; *obsequious fondness* dutiful affection, overdone deference **38**
in his reprieve in the interval before execution **39** *fitted* prepared **43** *remit*
pardon **44** *saucy sweetness* impudent enjoyment **44–45** *coin . . . forbid* i.e.,
counterfeit God's image using forbidden dies (here, unmarried women) **47**
mettle energy (punning on "metal"); *restrainèd means* forbidden methods

ISABELLA

49   'Tis set down so in heaven, but not in earth.

ANGELO

50   Say you so? Then I shall pose you quickly.
Which had you rather, that the most just law
Now took your brother's life, or to redeem him

53   Give up your body to such sweet uncleanness
As she that he hath stained?

ISABELLA   Sir, believe this,
I had rather give my body than my soul.

ANGELO

56   I talk not of your soul. Our compelled sins
57   Stand more for number than for account.

ISABELLA   How say you?

ANGELO

58   Nay, I'll not warrant that, for I can speak
Against the thing I say. Answer to this:

60   I, now the voice of the recorded law,
Pronounce a sentence on your brother's life.
Might there not be a charity in sin

63   To save this brother's life?

ISABELLA   Please you to do't,
I'll take it as a peril to my soul;
It is no sin at all, but charity.

ANGELO

Pleased you to do't, at peril of your soul,
67   Were equal poise of sin and charity.

ISABELLA

That I do beg his life, if it be sin,
Heaven let me bear it. You granting of my suit,
70   If that be sin, I'll make it my morn prayer

---

49 *'Tis . . . earth* i.e., heaven may regard begetting an illegitimate child as equivalent to murder, but the world does not   **50** *pose* put a difficult question to   **53** *sweet uncleanness* pleasurable defilement   **56** *compelled* constrained   **57** *Stand . . . account* i.e., go on the record, but don't count against us   **58** *warrant* stand by   **60** *recorded* written   **63** *Please* if it pleases   **67** *poise* balance

To have it added to the faults of mine
And nothing of your answer.   72

ANGELO   Nay, but hear me.
  Your sense pursues not mine. Either you are ignorant,   73
  Or seem so, crafty, and that's not good.   74

ISABELLA
  Let me be ignorant, and in nothing good
  But graciously to know I am no better.   76

ANGELO
  Thus wisdom wishes to appear most bright
  When it doth tax itself, as these black masks   78
  Proclaim an enshield beauty ten times louder   79
  Than beauty could, displayed. But mark me.   80
  To be receivèd plain, I'll speak more gross: 81
  Your brother is to die.

ISABELLA   So.

ANGELO
  And his offense is so, as it appears,
  Accountant to the law upon that pain.   85

ISABELLA   True.

ANGELO
  Admit no other way to save his life –
  As I subscribe not that, nor any other –   88
  But, in the loss of question, that you, his sister,   89
  Finding yourself desired of such a person   90
  Whose credit with the judge, or own great place,
  Could fetch your brother from the manacles   92
  Of the all-binding law, and that there were
  No earthly mean to save him, but that either
  You must lay down the treasures of your body
  To this supposed, or else to let him suffer,   96
  What would you do?

---

72 *nothing . . . answer* nothing for which you need answer   73 *ignorant* un-
comprehending   74 *crafty* craftily   76 *graciously* by God's grace   78 *tax* accuse   79 *enshield* hidden   81   *receivèd* understood   85   *Accountant*
accountable; *pain* penalty   88 *subscribe* assent to   89 *in . . . question* i.e., for
the sake of argument   92 *fetch* release   96 *supposed* imagined person

ISABELLA
As much for my poor brother as myself.
99 That is, were I under the terms of death,
100 Th' impression of keen whips I'd wear as rubies,
And strip myself to death as to a bed
102 That longing have been sick for, ere I'd yield
My body up to shame.
ANGELO Then must your brother die.
ISABELLA
And 'twere the cheaper way.
Better it were a brother died at once
Than that a sister, by redeeming him,
Should die for ever.
ANGELO
Were not you then as cruel as the sentence
That you have slandered so?
ISABELLA
110 Ignomy in ransom and free pardon
111 Are of two houses; lawful mercy
Is nothing kin to foul redemption.
ANGELO
You seemed of late to make the law a tyrant,
114 And rather proved the sliding of your brother
115 A merriment than a vice.
ISABELLA
O pardon me, my lord, it oft falls out
To have what we would have, we speak not what we
mean.
I something do excuse the thing I hate
For his advantage that I dearly love.
ANGELO
120 We are all frail.

---

99 *terms of death* death sentence 100 *impression* imprint 102 *longing . . . for* i.e., I have been sick with longing for 110 *Ignomy* ignominy 111 *of two houses* i.e., completely different 114 *sliding* moral dereliction 115 *merriment* prank

ISABELLA   Else let my brother die,
  If not a fedary, but only he   121
  Owe and succeed thy weakness.   122

ANGELO
  Nay, women are frail too.

ISABELLA
  Ay, as the glasses where they view themselves,
  Which are as easy broke as they make forms.   125
  Women, help heaven! Men their creation mar   126
  In profiting by them. Nay, call us ten times frail,
  For we are soft as our complexions are,   128
  And credulous to false prints.   129

ANGELO   I think it well,
  And from this testimony of your own sex –   *130*
  Since I suppose we are made to be no stronger   131
  Than faults may shake our frames – let me be bold.
  I do arrest your words. Be that you are,   133
  That is, a woman; if you be more, you're none.   134
  If you be one, as you are well expressed   135
  By all external warrants, show it now,   136
  By putting on the destined livery.   137

ISABELLA
  I have no tongue but one. Gentle my lord,   138
  Let me entreat you speak the former language.   139

ANGELO
  Plainly conceive, I love you.   *140*

---

121 *fedary* confederate   **122** *Owe . . . weakness* owns and inherits the frailty
you speak of (?)   **125** *make forms* produce images   **126–27** *Men . . . by
them* i.e., men ruin their own created excellence in exploiting frail women
128 *complexions* constitutions   **129** *credulous* susceptible; *prints* impressions;
I think it well that's what I think   **131** *I suppose* I take it   **131–32** *we . . . our
frames* i.e., we are not made so strong that we are invulnerable to evil   **133** *I
do arrest . . . words* i.e., I take you at your word; *that* that which   **134** *if you
be . . . none* i.e., if you're more than a woman, you aren't a woman   **135** *well
expressed* convincingly shown to be   **136** *external warrants* outward indica-
tions   **137** *destined livery* i.e., the garb of sexual service, to which all women
are destined   **138** *I . . . one* i.e., I can't do double-talk   **139** *former language*
i.e., previous plain language

ISABELLA
    My brother did love Juliet,
    And you tell me that he shall die for't.
ANGELO
    He shall not, Isabel, if you give me love.
ISABELLA
144   I know your virtue hath a license in't,
    Which seems a little fouler than it is,
146   To pluck on others.
ANGELO   Believe me, on mine honor,
    My words express my purpose.
ISABELLA
148   Ha! Little honor to be much believed,
    And most pernicious purpose. Seeming, seeming!
150   I will proclaim thee, Angelo, look for't!
151   Sign me a present pardon for my brother,
    Or with an outstretched throat I'll tell the world aloud
    What man thou art.
ANGELO   Who will believe thee, Isabel?
    My unsoiled name, th' austereness of my life,
155   My vouch against you, and my place i' th' state,
    Will so your accusation overweigh
157   That you shall stifle in your own report
    And smell of calumny. I have begun,
159   And now I give my sensual race the rein.
160   Fit thy consent to my sharp appetite,
161   Lay by all nicety and prolixious blushes,
162   That banish what they sue for. Redeem thy brother
    By yielding up thy body to my will,
    Or else he must not only die the death,
    But thy unkindness shall his death draw out

---

144 *license* allowed freedom 146 *pluck on others* trap people into self-betrayal 148 *Little . . . believed* i.e., you have little honor to warrant the extensive belief you solicit 150 *proclaim* denounce; *look for't* expect it 151 *present* immediate 155 *vouch* testimony 157 *report* story 159 *race* (1) steed, (2) speedy motion (?) 161 *nicety* delicacy, prissiness; *prolixious* prolonged (delaying) 162 *That . . . for* that reject what they really ask for

To ling'ring sufferance. Answer me tomorrow,   166
Or, by the affection that now guides me most,   167
I'll prove a tyrant to him. As for you,
Say what you can, my false o'erweighs your true.   *Exit.*

ISABELLA
To whom should I complain? Did I tell this,   170
Who would believe me? O perilous mouths,
That bear in them one and the selfsame tongue,
Either of condemnation or approof,   173
Bidding the law make curtsy to their will,   174
Hooking both right and wrong to th' appetite,
To follow as it draws. I'll to my brother.
Though he hath fall'n by prompture of the blood,   177
Yet hath he in him such a mind of honor
That, had he twenty heads to tender down   179
On twenty bloody blocks, he'd yield them up,   180
Before his sister should her body stoop
To such abhorred pollution.   182
Then, Isabel, live chaste, and, brother, die:
More than our brother is our chastity.
I'll tell him yet of Angelo's request,
And fit his mind to death, for his soul's rest.   *Exit.*

*

∽ **III.1**   *Enter Duke [as a friar], Claudio, and Provost.*

DUKE
So then you hope of pardon from Lord Angelo?

CLAUDIO
The miserable have no other medicine
But only hope.
I have hope to live, and am prepared to die.

---

166 *ling'ring sufferance* prolonged torment   167 *affection* feeling   170 *Did I
tell* if I were to tell   173 *approof* approval   174 *make curtsy* bow   177
prompture prompting   179 *tender* pay   182 *abhorred pollution* loathed defilement
III.1 The prison

DUKE
    Be absolute for death; either death or life
    Shall thereby be the sweeter. Reason thus with life:
    If I do lose thee, I do lose a thing
    That none but fools would keep. A breath thou art,
9   Servile to all the skyey influences
10   That dost this habitation where thou keep'st
11   Hourly afflict. Merely, thou art death's fool,
    For him thou labor'st by thy flight to shun,
    And yet run'st toward him still. Thou art not noble,
14   For all th' accommodations that thou bear'st
15   Are nursed by baseness. Thou'rt by no means valiant,
16   For thou dost fear the soft and tender fork
17   Of a poor worm. Thy best of rest is sleep,
18   And that thou oft provok'st, yet grossly fear'st
19   Thy death, which is no more. Thou art not thyself,
20   For thou exists on many a thousand grains
    That issue out of dust. Happy thou art not,
    For what thou hast not, still thou striv'st to get,
23   And what thou hast, forget'st. Thou art not certain,
24   For thy complexion shifts to strange effects,
    After the moon. If thou art rich, thou'rt poor,
26   For, like an ass whose back with ingots bows,
    Thou bear'st thy heavy riches but a journey,
    And death unloads thee. Friend hast thou none,
29   For thine own bowels, which do call thee sire,
30   The mere effusion of thy proper loins,
31   Do curse the gout, serpigo, and the rheum

---

9 *Servile . . . influences* i.e., subject to all the influences of the stars and planets 10 *keep'st* live 11 *Merely, thou art* you are no more than 14 *accommodations* creature comforts 15 *nursed by baseness* have base origins 16 *fork* forked tongue 17 *worm* snake; *thy best . . . is sleep* i.e., you are most tranquil when sleeping 18 *provok'st* call upon 19 *not thyself* i.e., not the whole man you think you are 20 *exists* subsist on; *grains* particles 23 *certain* constant 24–25 *thy complexion . . . moon* your disposition changes capriciously, as the moon changes 26 *ingots* bars of precious metal 29 *bowels* offspring 30 *The mere effusion* no more than the outpouring; *proper* own 31 *serpigo* skin eruption; *rheum* fluid discharge

For ending thee no sooner. Thou hast nor youth nor age,
But as it were an after-dinner's sleep,
Dreaming on both, for all thy blessèd youth
Becomes as agèd, and doth beg the alms   35
Of palsied eld; and when thou art old and rich,   36
Thou hast neither heat, affection, limb, nor beauty,   37
To make thy riches pleasant. What's yet in this
That bears the name of life? Yet in this life   39
Lie hid more thousand deaths; yet death we fear,   40
That makes these odds all even.
CLAUDIO   I humbly thank you.
To sue to live, I find I seek to die,   42
And, seeking death, find life. Let it come on.
    Enter Isabella.
ISABELLA
What, ho! Peace here, grace and good company.
PROVOST
Who's there? Come in, the wish deserves a welcome.
DUKE
Dear sir, ere long I'll visit you again.
CLAUDIO
Most holy sir, I thank you.
ISABELLA
My business is a word or two with Claudio.
PROVOST
And very welcome. Look, signor, here's your sister.
DUKE
Provost, a word with you.   50
PROVOST
As many as you please.
DUKE
Bring me to hear them speak, where I may be concealed.
    [Duke and Provost withdraw.]

----

35 *Becomes as agèd* is as dependent as old age (?)   36 *palsied eld* paralytic old
age   37 *heat* (sexual) energy; *affection* passion; *limb* bodily vitality   39
bears . . . life merits the name of life   42 *To sue* i.e., in suing

CLAUDIO
Now, sister, what's the comfort?
ISABELLA
Why,
As all comforts are, most good, most good indeed.
Lord Angelo, having affairs to heaven,
Intends you for his swift ambassador,
58 Where you shall be an everlasting leiger.
59 Therefore your best appointment make with speed;
60 Tomorrow you set on.
CLAUDIO   Is there no remedy?
ISABELLA
None but such remedy as, to save a head,
62 To cleave a heart in twain.
CLAUDIO   But is there any?
ISABELLA
Yes, brother, you may live.
There is a devilish mercy in the judge,
If you'll implore it, that will free your life,
66 But fetter you till death.
CLAUDIO   Perpetual durance?
ISABELLA
Ay, just – perpetual durance, a restraint,
68 Though all the world's vastidity you had,
69 To a determined scope.
CLAUDIO   But in what nature?
ISABELLA
70 In such a one as, you consenting to't,
71 Would bark your honor from that trunk you bear,
And leave you naked.
CLAUDIO   Let me know the point.

---

58 *leiger* resident ambassador   59 *appointment* preparation   60 *set on* depart
62 *cleave . . . in twain* cut in two   66 *fetter* manacle; *durance* imprisonment
68 *Though . . . vastidity* though you had all the world's vastness   69 *determined scope* restricted range; *in what nature* of what kind   71 *bark* strip

ISABELLA

O, I do fear thee, Claudio, and I quake,
Lest thou a feverous life shouldst entertain,   74
And six or seven winters more respect
Than a perpetual honor. Dar'st thou die?
The sense of death is most in apprehension,   77
And the poor beetle that we tread upon
In corporal sufferance finds a pang as great   79
As when a giant dies.   80

CLAUDIO   Why give you me this shame?
Think you I can a resolution fetch
From flow'ry tenderness? If I must die,   82
I will encounter darkness as a bride,
And hug it in mine arms.

ISABELLA

There spake my brother; there my father's grave
Did utter forth a voice. Yes, thou must die;
Thou art too noble to conserve a life
In base appliances. This outward-sainted deputy,   88
Whose settled visage and deliberate word   89
Nips youth i' th' head, and follies doth enew   90
As falcon doth the fowl, is yet a devil;   91
His filth within being cast, he would appear   92
A pond as deep as hell.   93

CLAUDIO   The prenzie Angelo?

ISABELLA

O, 'tis the cunning livery of hell,   94
The damnedest body to invest and cover
In prenzie guards! Dost thou think, Claudio,   96

---

74 *entertain* wish to maintain   77 *sense* painful experience; *apprehension* an-
ticipation   79 *corporal* bodily   80 *shame* mortification   82 *flow'ry* i.e., composed of figures of speech   88 *appliances* remedies; *outward-sainted* saintly
seeming   89 *settled visage* unyielding appearance   90 *enew* drive down into
the water   91 *fowl* bird   92 *cast* vomited forth   93, 96 *prenzie* (obscure)
94 *livery* servants' or retainers' uniform   96 *guards* trimmings; *Dost . . .
think* can you credit

If I would yield him my virginity,
Thou might'st be freed!
CLAUDIO   O heavens, it cannot be.
ISABELLA
99   Yes, he would give't thee, from this rank offense,
100 So to offend him still. This night's the time
     That I should do what I abhor to name,
     Or else thou diest tomorrow.
CLAUDIO   Thou shalt not do't.
ISABELLA
     O, were it but my life,
     I'd throw it down for your deliverance
105 As frankly as a pin.
CLAUDIO   Thanks, dear Isabel.
ISABELLA
     Be ready, Claudio, for your death tomorrow.
CLAUDIO
107 Yes. Has he affections in him,
108 That thus can make him bite the law by th' nose,
109 When he would force it? Sure it is no sin,
110 Or of the deadly seven it is the least.
ISABELLA
     Which is the least?
CLAUDIO
112 If it were damnable, he being so wise,
113 Why would he for the momentary trick
114 Be perdurably fined? O Isabel –
ISABELLA
     What says my brother?
CLAUDIO   Death is a fearful thing.
ISABELLA
     And shamèd life a hateful.

99–100 *he would . . . him still* i.e., from this squalid offense he would give
you means to sin again against his edict   105 *frankly* freely   107 *affections*
desires   108 *bite . . . nose* flout the law   109 *would force* should enforce
112 *were damnable* led to damnation   113 *trick* (1) trifle, (2) sexual act
114 *perdurably fined* punished eternally

CLAUDIO
　　Ay, but to die, and go we know not where,
　　To lie in cold obstruction and to rot,   118
　　This sensible warm motion to become   119
　　A kneaded clod; and the delighted spirit   120
　　To bathe in fiery floods, or to reside
　　In thrilling region of thick-ribbèd ice,   122
　　To be imprisoned in the viewless winds   123
　　And blown with restless violence round about
　　The pendent world; or to be worse than worst   125
　　Of those that lawless and incertain thought   126
　　Imagine howling, 'tis too horrible.
　　The weariest and most loathèd worldly life
　　That age, ache, penury, and imprisonment
　　Can lay on nature is a paradise   130
　　To what we fear of death.
ISABELLA
　　Alas, alas.
CLAUDIO   Sweet sister, let me live.
　　What sin you do to save a brother's life,
　　Nature dispenses with the deed so far   134
　　That it becomes a virtue.
ISABELLA   O you beast,
　　O faithless coward, O dishonest wretch!
　　Wilt thou be made a man out of my vice?
　　Is't not a kind of incest, to take life
　　From thine own sister's shame? What should I think?
　　Heaven shield my mother played my father fair,   140
　　For such a warpèd slip of wilderness   141
　　Ne'er issued from his blood. Take my defiance,
　　Die, perish. Might but my bending down

---

118 *obstruction* constriction **119** *sensible* sentient; *motion* body **120** *kneaded clod* practically shapeless lump of clay; *delighted* capable of delight **122** *thrilling* piercingly cold; *thick-ribbèd* densely packed in ridges **123** *viewless* invisible **125** *pendent* suspended in space **126** *incertain* conjectural **134** *dispenses* pardons **140** *shield* forbid **141** *warpèd . . . wilderness* i.e., wild, deviant shoot (bastard)

Reprieve thee from thy fate, it should proceed.
I'll pray a thousand prayers for thy death,
No word to save thee.

CLAUDIO
Nay, hear me, Isabel.

ISABELLA   O, fie, fie, fie!
148 Thy sin's not accidental, but a trade;
Mercy to thee would prove itself a bawd,
150 'Tis best that thou diest quickly.   *[Going]*

CLAUDIO   O hear me, Isabella.

[Duke comes forward.]

DUKE
151 Vouchsafe a word, young sister, but one word.

ISABELLA   What is your will?

DUKE   Might you dispense with your leisure, I would by
154   and by have some speech with you. The satisfaction I
would require is likewise your own benefit.

ISABELLA   I have no superfluous leisure; my stay must be
157   stolen out of other affairs, but I will attend you a while.

DUKE   *[Aside to Claudio]* Son, I have overheard what
hath passed between you and your sister. Angelo had
160   never the purpose to corrupt her; only he hath made an
161   assay of her virtue to practice his judgment with the
disposition of natures. She, having the truth of honor
in her, hath made him that gracious denial which he is
most glad to receive. I am confessor to Angelo, and I
know this to be true; therefore prepare yourself to
166   death. Do not satisfy your resolution with hopes that
are fallible; tomorrow you must die. Go to your knees
and make ready.

CLAUDIO   Let me ask my sister pardon. I am so out of
170   love with life that I will sue to be rid of it.

---

148 *accidental* a chance occurrence   151 *Vouchsafe* grant   154 *satisfaction*
result   157 *attend* wait for   161 *assay* trial   161–62 *to practice ... natures*
test his judgment of character   166 *satisfy* compromise

DUKE   Hold you there. Farewell.   *[Exit Claudio.]*
          [Enter Provost.]
     Provost, a word with you.
PROVOST   What's your will, father?
DUKE   That now you are come, you will be gone. Leave
     me a while with the maid; my mind promises with my   175
     habit no loss shall touch her by my company.
PROVOST   In good time.   *Exit.*
DUKE   The hand that hath made you fair hath made you
     good. The goodness that is cheap in beauty makes   179
     beauty brief in goodness, but grace, being the soul of 180
     your complexion, shall keep the body of it ever fair.
     The assault that Angelo hath made to you, fortune
     hath conveyed to my understanding; and, but that
     frailty hath examples for his falling, I should wonder at 184
     Angelo. How will you do to content this substitute,
     and to save your brother?
ISABELLA   I am now going to resolve him. I had rather   187
     my brother die by the law than my son should be un-
     lawfully born. But O, how much is the good duke de-
     ceived in Angelo! If ever he return and I can speak to   *190*
     him, I will open my lips in vain, or discover his govern- 191
     ment.
DUKE   That shall not be much amiss. Yet, as the matter
     now stands, he will avoid your accusation; he made   194
     trial of you only. Therefore fasten your ear on my advis-
     ings: to the love I have in doing good a remedy presents
     itself. I do make myself believe that you may most up-
     righteously do a poor wronged lady a merited benefit,
     redeem your brother from the angry law, do no stain to
     your own gracious person, and much please the absent   *200*

175–76 *my mind . . . my habit* my state of mind promises as much as my
habit   179–80 *cheap . . . in goodness* i.e., beauty devoid of goodness will be
short-lived (?)   180 *grace* God-given goodness   180–81 *soul . . . complexion*
essence of your makeup   184 *examples* precedents   187 *resolve* answer   191
discover expose   191–92 *government* conduct   194 *avoid* circumvent

201 duke, if peradventure he shall ever return to have hearing of this business.

ISABELLA   Let me hear you speak farther. I have spirit to
do anything that appears not foul in the truth of my
spirit.

DUKE   Virtue is bold, and goodness never fearful. Have
you not heard speak of Mariana, the sister of Frederick,
208 the great soldier, who miscarried at sea?

ISABELLA   I have heard of the lady, and good words went
210 with her name.

211 DUKE   She should this Angelo have married, was affi-
212 anced by her oath, and the nuptial appointed. Between
213 which time of the contract and limit of the solemnity,
214 her brother Frederick was wracked at sea, having in that
perished vessel the dowry of his sister. But mark how
heavily this befell to the poor gentlewoman. There she
lost a noble and renowned brother, in his love toward
her ever most kind and natural; with him the portion
and sinew of her fortune, her marriage dowry; with
220 both, her combinate husband, this well-seeming Angelo.

ISABELLA   Can this be so? Did Angelo so leave her?

DUKE   Left her in her tears, and dried not one of them
224 with his comfort; swallowed his vows whole, pretend-
225 ing in her discoveries of dishonor; in few, bestowed her
on her own lamentation, which she yet wears for his
227 sake; and he, a marble to her tears, is washed with
them, but relents not.

ISABELLA   What a merit were it in death to take this poor
230 maid from the world! What corruption in this life, that

---

201 *peradventure* perchance   208 *miscarried* came to grief   211–12 *affianced* betrothed   212 *nuptial appointed* marriage arranged   213 *limit . . .
solemnity* date set for the wedding   214 *wracked* wrecked   220 *combinate*
betrothed   224–25 *pretending . . . dishonor* i.e., alleging evidence of sexual
misconduct on her part   225–26 *bestowed . . . lamentation* gave her in "marriage" to her own mourning (garb)   227 *a marble* (1) marble, (2) a monument

it will let this man live! But how out of this can she
avail?   232

DUKE   It is a rupture that you may easily heal; and the
cure of it not only saves your brother, but keeps you
from dishonor in doing it.

ISABELLA   Show me how, good father.

DUKE   This forenamed maid hath yet in her the continuance of her first affection. His unjust unkindness, that
in all reason should have quenched her love, hath, like
an impediment in the current, made it more violent   240
and unruly. Go you to Angelo, answer his requiring   241
with a plausible obedience, agree with his demands to   242
the point. Only refer yourself to this advantage: first, 243
that your stay with him may not be long, that the time
may have all shadow and silence in it, and the place an- 245
swer to convenience. This being granted in course –   246
and now follows all – we shall advise this wronged
maid to stead up your appointment, go in your place. If 248
the encounter acknowledge itself hereafter, it may com- 249
pel him to her recompense; and here, by this is your   250
brother saved, your honor untainted, the poor Mariana
advantaged, and the corrupt deputy scaled. The maid   252
will I frame and make fit for his attempt. If you think   253
well to carry this, as you may, the doubleness of the   254
benefit defends the deceit from reproof. What think
you of it?

ISABELLA   The image of it gives me content already, and I
trust it will grow to a most prosperous perfection.   258

DUKE   It lies much in your holding up. Haste you speed- 259
ily to Angelo. If for this night he entreat you to his bed, 260

---

232 *avail* benefit   241 *requiring* demand   242 *plausible* complaisant
242–43 *to the point* punctiliously   243 *refer . . . advantage* i.e., request him
to meet these conditions   245 *shadow and silence* darkness and secrecy
245–46 *answer . . . convenience* suit your convenience   246 *in course* in due
course   248 *stead up* go instead to   249 *acknowledge itself* becomes public
252 *scaled* weighed in the balance   253 *frame* prepare   254 *carry* conduct
258 *perfection* conclusion   259 *holding up* management

give him promise of satisfaction. I will presently to
262   Saint Luke's; there at the moated grange resides this de-
jected Mariana. At that place call upon me, and dispatch with Angelo, that it may be quickly.

ISABELLA   I thank you for this comfort. Fare you well,
good father.   *Exit.*

∗

∾ **III.2** *Enter Elbow, Clown [Pompey], Officers.*

ELBOW   Nay, if there be no remedy for it but that you
will needs buy and sell men and women like beasts, we
3   shall have all the world drink brown and white bastard.

DUKE   O heavens, what stuff is here?

5   POMPEY   'Twas never merry world since, of two usuries,
the merriest was put down, and the worser allowed by
7   order of law a furred gown to keep him warm – and
furred with fox and lamb skins too, to signify that craft,
9   being richer than innocency, stands for the facing.

10   ELBOW   Come your way, sir. Bless you, good father friar.

DUKE   And you, good brother father. What offense hath
this man made you, sir?

ELBOW   Marry, sir, he hath offended the law; and, sir, we
take him to be a thief too, sir, for we have found upon
him, sir, a strange picklock, which we have sent to the
deputy.

DUKE
Fie, sirrah, a bawd, a wicked bawd!
The evil that thou causest to be done,
That is thy means to live. Do thou but think
20   What 'tis to cram a maw or clothe a back
From such a filthy vice; say to thyself,

---

262 *moated grange* country house surrounded by a moat
III.2 The prison **3** *bastard* sweet Spanish wine (with obvious pun) **5**
two usuries i.e., prostitution and moneylending at interest, both "unnatural"
7 *order of law* statute **9** *stands for the facing* i.e., can afford these trimmings
20 *maw* stomach

From their abominable and beastly touches   22
I drink, I eat, array myself, and live.
Canst thou believe thy living is a life,
So stinkingly depending? Go mend, go mend.   25
POMPEY   Indeed, it does stink in some sort, sir, but yet,
sir, I would prove –
DUKE
Nay, if the devil have given thee proofs for sin,   28
Thou wilt prove his. Take him to prison, officer.   29
Correction and instruction must both work   30
Ere this rude beast will profit.
ELBOW   He must before the deputy, sir; he has given him
warning. The deputy cannot abide a whoremaster; if he
be a whoremonger, and comes before him, he were as   34
good go a mile on his errand.
DUKE
That we were all, as some would seem to be,   36
Free from our faults, as faults from seeming free!
     Enter Lucio.
ELBOW   His neck will come to your waist – a cord, sir.   38
POMPEY   I spy comfort, I cry bail. Here's a gentleman
and a friend of mine.   40
LUCIO   How now, noble Pompey? What, at the wheels of   41
Caesar? Art thou led in triumph? What, is there none
of Pygmalion's images newly made woman to be had   43
now, for putting the hand in the pocket and extracting
it clutched? What reply, ha? What sayst thou to this
tune, matter, and method? Is't not drowned i' th' last   46

---

22 *touches* sexual encounters   25 *depending* dependent   28 *proofs for sin* arguments in favor of sin   29 *prove his* prove yourself his own   30 *Correction* punishment   34–35 *he were . . . errand* i.e., he is in for some hard going (?)   36–37 *That . . . free* i.e., if only we were all actually as free from fault as some hypocrites appear to be (?)   38 *His neck . . . your waist* i.e., like your waist, his neck will have a cord around it   41–42 *the wheels of Caesar* Caesar's chariot (behind which Pompey is being drawn)   43 *Pygmalion's images* i.e., prostitutes (fresh, beautiful women created by art, as in Ovid's *Metamorphoses,* where Pygmalion's sculpture of Galatea comes to life)   46 *tune* tone; *method* manner of speaking   46–47 *Is't not . . . rain* (uncertain)

47   rain, ha? What sayst thou, trot? Is the world as it was,
48   man? Which is the way? Is it sad, and few words, or
49   how? The trick of it?
50 DUKE   Still thus, and thus, still worse.

LUCIO   How doth my dear morsel, thy mistress? Procures
she still, ha?

53 POMPEY   Troth, sir, she hath eaten up all her beef, and
54   she is herself in the tub.

LUCIO   Why, 'tis good. It is the right of it; it must be so.
56   Ever your fresh whore and your powdered bawd, an
57   unshunned consequence; it must be so. Art going to
prison, Pompey?

POMPEY   Yes, faith, sir.

60 LUCIO   Why, 'tis not amiss, Pompey; farewell. Go, say I
sent thee thither. For debt, Pompey, or how?

ELBOW   For being a bawd, for being a bawd.

LUCIO   Well, then, imprison him. If imprisonment be
64   the due of a bawd, why, 'tis his right. Bawd is he doubt-
65   less, and of antiquity too: bawd-born. Farewell, good
Pompey; commend me to the prison, Pompey. You will
67   turn good husband now, Pompey, you will keep the
house.

POMPEY   I hope, sir, your good worship will be my bail.

70 LUCIO   No, indeed will I not, Pompey, it is not the wear.
I will pray, Pompey, to increase your bondage; if you
72   take it not patiently, why, your mettle is the more.
Adieu, trusty Pompey. Bless you, friar.

DUKE   And you.

75 LUCIO   Does Bridget paint still, Pompey, ha?

---

47 *trot* old crone   48 *sad* unhappy, morose   49 *trick* manner   50 *thus, and thus* i.e., on and on he goes in the same way   53 *eaten . . . beef* (1) used up all her whores (?), (2) run out of sustenance   54 *in the tub* i.e., getting treated for syphilis by exposure to mercury vapor   56 *powdered* (1) pickled in a tub, (2) covered with face powder   57 *unshunned consequence* unavoidable result   64–65 *doubtless* undoubtedly   65 *of antiquity* of old   67–68 *keep the house* stay indoors   70 *not the wear* not in style now   72 *mettle* spirit (punning on "metal")   75 *paint* wear makeup

ELBOW   Come your ways, sir, come.

POMPEY   You will not bail me then, sir?

LUCIO   Then, Pompey, nor now. What news abroad, friar, what news?

ELBOW   Come your ways, sir, come.   *80*

LUCIO   Go to kennel, Pompey, go.

            [Exeunt Elbow, Pompey, and Officers.]
        What news, friar, of the duke?

DUKE   I know none. Can you tell me of any?

LUCIO   Some say he is with the emperor of Russia; other   *84*
some, he is in Rome. But where is he, think you?

DUKE   I know not where, but wheresoever, I wish him well.

LUCIO   It was a mad fantastical trick of him to steal from the state, and usurp the beggary he was never born to. Lord Angelo dukes it well in his absence; he puts trans-   *90* gression to't.

DUKE   He does well in't.   *92*

LUCIO   A little more lenity to lechery would do no harm in him. Something too crabbed that way, friar.   *94*

DUKE   It is too general a vice, and severity must cure it.

LUCIO   Yes, in good sooth, the vice is of a great kindred,   *96* it is well allied; but it is impossible to extirp it quite,   *97* friar, till eating and drinking be put down. They say this Angelo was not made by man and woman after this downright way of creation. Is it true, think you?   *100*

DUKE   How should he be made then?

LUCIO   Some report a sea-maid spawned him; some that   *102* he was begot between two stockfishes. But it is certain   *103* that when he makes water his urine is congealed ice, that I know to be true. And he is a motion genera-   *105* tive, that's infallible.   *106*

84–85 *other some* others   **92** *He . . . in't* he does well in doing so   **94** *crabbed* harsh   **96** *of a great kindred* (1) well connected, (2) has a large family   **97** *extirp* extirpate   **100** *downright* down-to-earth   **102** *sea-maid* mermaid   **103** *stockfishes* dried cod   **105–6** *motion generative* masculine puppet   **106** *infallible* certain

107 DUKE   You are pleasant, sir, and speak apace.

       LUCIO   Why, what a ruthless thing is this in him, for the
109   rebellion of a codpiece to take away the life of a man!
110 Would the duke that is absent have done this? Ere he
111   would have hanged a man for the getting a hundred
       bastards, he would have paid for the nursing a thou-
       sand. He had some feeling of the sport, he knew the
114   service, and that instructed him to mercy.

115 DUKE   I never heard the absent duke much detected for
       women. He was not inclined that way.

       LUCIO   O, sir, you are deceived.

       DUKE   'Tis not possible.

119 LUCIO   Who? Not the duke? Yes, your beggar of fifty,
120   and his use was to put a ducat in her clackdish. The
121   duke had crotchets in him. He would be drunk, too;
       that let me inform you.

       DUKE   You do him wrong, surely.

124 LUCIO   Sir, I was an inward of his. A shy fellow was the
125   duke, and I believe I know the cause of his withdraw-
       ing.

       DUKE   What, I prithee, might be the cause?

       LUCIO   No, pardon. 'Tis a secret must be locked within
       the teeth and the lips. But this I can let you under-
130   stand: the greater file of the subject held the duke to be
       wise.

       DUKE   Wise? Why, no question but he was.

133 LUCIO   A very superficial, ignorant, unweighing fellow.

       DUKE   Either this is envy in you, folly, or mistaking. The
135   very stream of his life and the business he hath helmed

---

107 *pleasant* facetious; *speak apace* run off your mouth   **109** *codpiece*
padding or device worn by a man to simulate a large penis (here, meaning
penis)   **111** *getting* begetting   **114** *service* sexual trade   **115** *detected* accused   **119** *beggar of fifty* fifty-year-old beggarwoman   **120** *clackdish*
wooden begging bowl (with sexual innuendo)   **121** *crotchets* strange whims
124 *inward* intimate   **125–26** *withdrawing* absenting himself   **130** *greater
file* most people   **133** *unweighing* unreflecting   **135** *stream* regular course;
helmed steered

must, upon a warranted need, give him a better proc-   136
lamation. Let him be but testimonied in his own   137
bringings-forth, and he shall appear to the envious a
scholar, a statesman, and a soldier. Therefore you speak
unskillfully, or, if your knowledge be more, it is much   140
darkened in your malice.

LUCIO   Sir, I know him, and I love him.

DUKE   Love talks with better knowledge, and knowledge
with dearer love.

LUCIO   Come, sir, I know what I know.

DUKE   I can hardly believe that, since you know not
what you speak. But if ever the duke return, as our
prayers are he may, let me desire you to make your an-   148
swer before him. If it be honest you have spoke, you
have courage to maintain it. I am bound to call upon   150
you, and, I pray you, your name?

LUCIO   Sir, my name is Lucio, well known to the duke.

DUKE   He shall know you better, sir, if I may live to report you.

LUCIO   I fear you not.

DUKE   O, you hope the duke will return no more, or you
imagine me too unhurtful an opposite, but indeed I   157
can do you little harm; you'll forswear this again.   158

LUCIO   I'll be hanged first; thou art deceived in me, friar.
But no more of this. Canst thou tell if Claudio die to-   *160*
morrow or no?

DUKE   Why should he die, sir?

LUCIO   Why? For filling a bottle with a tundish. I would   163
the duke we talk of were returned again. This ungeni-   164
tured agent will unpeople the province with conti-
nency. Sparrows must not build in his house eaves
because they are lecherous. The duke yet would have

---

136 *warranted* authentic   **136–37** *proclamation* report   **137–38** *testimonied . . . bringings-forth* i.e., let his own accomplishments attest   **140** *unskillfully* ignorantly   **148–49** *make your answer* justify your allegations   **150**
call upon summon   **157** *opposite* opponent   **158** *forswear* deny   **163**
tundish funnel   **164–65** *ungenitured* without genitals

168   dark deeds darkly answered; he would never bring
      them to light. Would he were returned. Marry, this
170   Claudio is condemned for untrussing. Farewell, good
      friar; I prithee, pray for me. The duke, I say to thee
172   again, would eat mutton on Fridays. He's now past it;
173   yet – and I say to thee – he could mouth with a beggar,
      though she smelt brown bread and garlic. Say that I
      said so; farewell.   *Exit.*

DUKE
      No might nor greatness in mortality
      Can censure scape. Back-wounding calumny
      The whitest virtue strikes. What king so strong
179   Can tie the gall up in the slanderous tongue?
180   But who comes here?
          Enter Escalus, Provost, and [Officers with] Bawd
          [Mistress Overdone].

ESCALUS   Go, away with her to prison.

MISTRESS OVERDONE   Good my lord, be good to me.
      Your honor is accounted a merciful man, good my lord.

184   ESCALUS   Double and treble admonition, and still forfeit
      in the same kind! This would make mercy swear, and
      play the tyrant.

PROVOST   A bawd of eleven years' continuance, may it
      please your honor.

189   MISTRESS OVERDONE   My lord, this is one Lucio's infor-
190   mation against me. Mistress Kate Keepdown was with
      child by him in the duke's time; he promised her mar-
192   riage. His child is a year and a quarter old, come Philip
      and Jacob. I have kept it myself, and see how he goes
      about to abuse me.

ESCALUS   That fellow is a fellow of much license; let him
      be called before us. Away with her to prison; go to, no

---

168 *dark deeds . . . answered* secret (sexual) misdeeds dealt with secretly
170 *untrussing* removing his breeches 172 *mutton* prostitute 173 *mouth
with* kiss 179 *gall* bitterness 184 *admonition* warning 184–85 *still forfeit . . . kind* still culpable for the same offense 189–90 *information* accusation 192–93 *Philip and Jacob* the feast of Saints Philip and James (May 1)

more words. *[Exeunt Officers with Mistress Overdone.]*
Provost, my brother Angelo will not be altered; Claudio must die tomorrow. Let him be furnished with di-   199
vines, and have all charitable preparation. If my brother   *200*
wrought by my pity, it should not be so with him.

PROVOST   So please you, this friar hath been with him,
and advised him for th' entertainment of death.   203

ESCALUS   Good even, good father.

DUKE   Bliss and goodness on you!

ESCALUS   Of whence are you?

DUKE
Not of this country, though my chance is now
To use it for my time. I am a brother
Of gracious order, late come from the see,   209
In special business from his holiness.   210

ESCALUS   What news abroad i' th' world?

DUKE   None, but that there is so great a fever on good-   212
ness that the dissolution of it must cure it. Novelty is   213
only in request, and it is as dangerous to be aged in any   214
kind of course as it is virtuous to be constant in any un-
dertaking. There is scarce truth enough alive to make
societies secure, but security enough to make fellow-   217
ships accursed. Much upon this riddle runs the wisdom
of the world. This news is old enough, yet it is every
day's news. I pray you, sir, of what disposition was the   *220*
duke?

ESCALUS   One that, above all other strifes, contended es-   222
pecially to know himself.

DUKE   What pleasure was he given to?

ESCALUS   Rather rejoicing to see another merry, than
merry at anything which professed to make him re-   226

199–200 *furnished with divines* provided with clergy   203 *entertainment* re-
ception   209 *see* i.e., Rome, the seat of the papacy   210 *his holiness* the pope
212–13 *fever on goodness* i.e., goodness is so sick   213 *dissolution* death
214 *in request* in demand   214–15 *aged . . . course* steady in any undertak-
ing   217–18 *security . . . accursed* i.e., enough misplaced trust to make social
relations accursed (?)   222 *strifes* efforts   226 *professed* attempted

joice: a gentleman of all temperance. But leave we him
228 to his events, with a prayer they may prove prosperous,
and let me desire to know how you find Claudio pre-
230 pared. I am made to understand that you have lent him
visitation.
232 DUKE   He professes to have received no sinister measure
from his judge, but most willingly humbles himself to
234 the determination of justice. Yet had he framed to himself, by the instruction of his frailty, many deceiving
promises of life, which I, by my good leisure, have discredited to him, and now is he resolved to die.
ESCALUS   You have paid the heavens your function, and
the prisoner the very debt of your calling. I have la-
240 bored for the poor gentleman to the extremest shore of
my modesty, but my brother justice have I found so severe that he hath forced me to tell him he is indeed justice.
244 DUKE   If his own life answer the straitness of his proceed-
ing, it shall become him well; wherein if he chance to
fail, he hath sentenced himself.
ESCALUS   I am going to visit the prisoner. Fare you well.
                              [Exeunt Escalus and Provost.]
DUKE   Peace be with you!
          He who the sword of heaven will bear
250   Should be as holy as severe;
251   Pattern in himself to know,
252   Grace to stand, and virtue go;
253   More nor less to others paying
          Than by self-offenses weighing.
          Shame to him whose cruel striking
          Kills for faults of his own liking.

---

228 *events* affairs   230–31 *lent . . . visitation* visited him   232 *sinister mea-*
sure unjust verdict   234 *framed* conceived   240–41 *extremest shore . . .*
modesty to the limit of propriety   244 *straitness* strictness   251 *Pattern . . .*
know be conscious of himself as a model   252 *Grace . . . go* God's grace to be
steadfast, and virtue to act   253–54 *More . . . weighing* inflicting no more
nor less on others than his own offenses warrant

Twice treble shame on Angelo,
To weed my vice and let his grow.
O, what may man within him hide,
Though angel on the outward side!   *260*
How may likeness made in crimes,   *261*
Making practice on the times,   *262*
To draw with idle spider's strings
Most ponderous and substantial things?   *264*
Craft against vice I must apply;
With Angelo tonight shall lie
His old betrothèd, but despisèd:
So disguise shall by th' disguisèd
Pay with falsehood, false exacting,   *269*
And perform an old contracting.   *Exit.*   *270*

                              *

∾ **IV.1** *Enter Mariana, and Boy singing.*

Song.
Take, O take those lips away,
    That so sweetly were forsworn;
And those eyes, the break of day,
    Lights that do mislead the morn;   *4*
But my kisses bring again, bring again,
Seals of love, but sealed in vain, sealed in vain.

    Enter Duke [disguised as before].
MARIANA
Break off thy song, and haste thee quick away.
Here comes a man of comfort, whose advice
Hath often stilled my brawling discontent. *[Exit Boy.]*   *9*
I cry you mercy, sir, and well could wish   *10*

———
261 *likeness . . . crimes* (obscure, but suggesting hypocrisy) **262** *practice* deception **264** *ponderous* weighty **269** *exacting* exaction
  IV.1 The moated grange **4** *mislead the morn* falsely promise dawn (?) **9** *brawling* clamorous

You had not found me here so musical.
Let me excuse me, and believe me so,
13   My mirth it much displeased, but pleased my woe.
DUKE
        'Tis good, though music oft hath such a charm
        To make bad good, and good provoke to harm.
        I pray you tell me, hath anybody inquired for me here
        today? Much upon this time have I promised here to
        meet.
MARIANA   You have not been inquired after. I have sat
20   here all day.
            Enter Isabella.
21 DUKE   I do constantly believe you. The time is come even
        now. I shall crave your forbearance a little; may be I will
        call upon you anon, for some advantage to yourself.
MARIANA   I am always bound to you.   *Exit.*
DUKE
        Very well met, and welcome.
        What is the news from this good deputy?
ISABELLA
27   He hath a garden circummured with brick,
        Whose western side is with a vineyard backed;
29   And to that vineyard is a planchèd gate,
30   That makes his opening with this bigger key.
31   This other doth command a little door
        Which from the vineyard to the garden leads.
        There have I made my promise,
        Upon the heavy middle of the night,
        To call upon him.
DUKE
36   But shall you on your knowledge find this way?

---

13 *My mirth . . . woe* i.e., it conflicted with (my) good spirits but gratified
my sadness 21 *constantly* firmly 27 *circummured* walled about 29
planchèd made of planks 30 *makes his opening* is opened 31 *command*
control 36 *on your knowledge* i.e., from what you have been told

ISABELLA

   I have ta'en a due and wary note upon't.   37

   With whispering and most guilty diligence,

   In action all of precept, he did show me   39

   The way twice o'er.   40

DUKE   Are there no other tokens

   Between you 'greed concerning her observance?   41

ISABELLA

   No, none, but only a repair i' th' dark,   42

   And that I have possessed him my most stay   43

   Can be but brief; for I have made him know

   I have a servant comes with me along,

   That stays upon me, whose persuasion is   46

   I come about my brother.   47

DUKE   'Tis well borne up.

   I have not yet made known to Mariana

   A word of this. What ho, within! Come forth!

     Enter Mariana.

   I pray you, be acquainted with this maid;   50

   She comes to do you good.   51

ISABELLA   I do desire the like.

DUKE

   Do you persuade yourself that I respect you?

MARIANA

   Good friar, I know you do, and have found it.

DUKE

   Take then this your companion by the hand,

   Who hath a story ready for your ear.

   I shall attend your leisure, but make haste;   56

   The vaporous night approaches.   57

---

37 *wary* attentive **39** *In action . . . precept* teaching by demonstration **40** *tokens* signs **41** *observance* prescribed conduct **42** *repair* visit **43** *possessed* informed **46** *stays upon* waits for; *persuasion* belief **47** *borne up* sustained **51** *the like* the same **56** *attend . . . your leisure* wait until you have finished and are free again **57** *vaporous* damp

MARIANA
    Will't please you walk aside?
                  Exeunt [Mariana and Isabella].

DUKE
    O place and greatness, millions of false eyes

60   Are stuck upon thee. Volumes of report
61   Run with these false, and most contrarious quest
62   Upon thy doings. Thousand escapes of wit
63   Make thee the father of their idle dream,
64   And rack thee in their fancies.
    Enter Mariana and Isabella.
                     Welcome, how agreed?

ISABELLA
    She'll take the enterprise upon her, father,
66   If you advise it.

DUKE   It is not my consent,
    But my entreaty too.

ISABELLA   Little have you to say
    When you depart from him but, soft and low,
69   "Remember now my brother."

MARIANA   Fear me not.

DUKE
70   Nor, gentle daughter, fear you not at all;
71   He is your husband on a precontract;
    To bring you thus together, 'tis no sin,
73   Sith that the justice of your title to him
74   Doth flourish the deceit. Come, let us go;
75   Our corn's to reap, for yet our tithe's to sow.   *Exeunt.*

                         *

---

61 *most contrarious quest* i.e., scrutinize (hunt down) with the utmost perversity and ill will   **62** *escapes* sallies   **63** *Make . . . dream* i.e., make you the source and subject of their frivolous imaginings   **64** *rack* distort, misconstrue   **66** *not* not only   **69** *Fear me not* you can rely on me   **70** *fear you not* don't doubt   **71** *precontract* legally binding proposal   **73** *Sith* since   **74** *flourish* embellish   **75** *corn's to reap . . . sow* i.e., we still have to sow before we can reap the corn; *our tithe* our share (?)

∾ **IV.2** *Enter Provost and Clown [Pompey].*

PROVOST　Come hither, sirrah. Can you cut off a man's 1
head?

POMPEY　If the man be a bachelor, sir, I can; but if he be
a married man, he's his wife's head, and I can never cut 4
off a woman's head.

PROVOST　Come, sir, leave me your snatches, and yield 6
me a direct answer. Tomorrow morning are to die
Claudio and Barnardine. Here is in our prison a common executioner, who in his office lacks a helper. If you
will take it on you to assist him, it shall redeem you 10
from your gyves; if not, you shall have your full time of 11
imprisonment, and your deliverance with an unpitied 12
whipping, for you have been a notorious bawd.

POMPEY　Sir, I have been an unlawful bawd time out of
mind, but yet I will be content to be a lawful hangman.
I would be glad to receive some instruction from my
fellow partner.

PROVOST　What ho, Abhorson! Where's Abhorson there?
Enter Abhorson.

ABHORSON　Do you call, sir?

PROVOST　Sirrah, here's a fellow will help you tomorrow 20
in your execution. If you think it meet, compound 21
with him by the year, and let him abide here with you;
if not, use him for the present and dismiss him. He
cannot plead his estimation with you; he hath been a 24
bawd.

ABHORSON　A bawd, sir? Fie upon him, he will discredit
our mystery. 27

PROVOST　Go to, sir, you weigh equally; a feather will
turn the scale.　　　　　　　　　　　　　　　　*Exit.*

IV.2 The prison　**1** *sirrah* you, sir (mode of address to an inferior)　**4** *his
wife's head* i.e., her superior, according to biblical precept　**6** *snatches* quips
11 *gyves* fetters　**12** *unpitied* merciless　**21** *compound* make an agreement
24 *estimation* good character, reputation　**27** *mystery* craft, calling

30 POMPEY   Pray, sir, by your good favor – for surely, sir, a
31   good favor you have, but that you have a hanging
   look – do you call, sir, your occupation a mystery?
ABHORSON   Ay, sir, a mystery.
34 POMPEY   Painting, sir, I have heard say, is a mystery, and
35   your whores, sir, being members of my occupation,
   using painting, do prove my occupation a mystery. But
   what mystery there should be in hanging, if I should be
   hanged, I cannot imagine.
ABHORSON   Sir, it is a mystery.
40 POMPEY   Proof?
41 ABHORSON   Every true man's apparel fits your thief.
42 POMPEY   If it be too little for your thief, your true man
   thinks it big enough. If it be too big for your thief, your
   thief thinks it little enough; so every true man's apparel
   fits your thief.
     Enter Provost.
PROVOST   Are you agreed?
POMPEY   Sir, I will serve him, for I do find your hangman
   is a more penitent trade than your bawd; he doth of-
49   tener ask forgiveness.
50 PROVOST   You, sirrah, provide your block and your ax tomorrow four o'clock.
ABHORSON   Come on, bawd. I will instruct thee in my
   trade; follow.
POMPEY   I do desire to learn, sir; and I hope, if you have
55   occasion to use me for your own turn, you shall find
56   me yare. For truly, sir, for your kindness I owe you a
   good turn.
PROVOST
   Call hither Barnardine and Claudio.
                    Exeunt [Pompey and Abhorson].

---

31 *favor* face   34 *Painting* the art of painting (here implying the application
of cosmetics)   35 *your whores* i.e., whores in general   41 *true* honest
42–43 *If . . . enough* (uncertain)   49 *ask forgiveness* (hangmen asked to be
forgiven by those they were about to execute)   55 *for . . . turn* for your own
execution   56 *yare* ready

Th' one has my pity, not a jot the other,
Being a murderer, though he were my brother.   60
    Enter Claudio.
Look, here's the warrant, Claudio, for thy death.
'Tis now dead midnight, and by eight tomorrow
Thou must be made immortal. Where's Barnardine?
CLAUDIO
As fast locked up in sleep as guiltless labor
When it lies starkly in the traveler's bones.   65
He will not wake.   66
PROVOST   Who can do good on him?
Well, go, prepare yourself.
    [Knocking within.]   But hark, what noise?
Heaven give your spirits comfort.   *[Exit Claudio.]*
                        By and by!
I hope it is some pardon or reprieve
For the most gentle Claudio.   70
    Enter Duke [disguised as before].
                   Welcome, father.
DUKE
The best and wholesom'st spirits of the night
Envelop you, good provost. Who called here of late?
PROVOST
None since the curfew rung.   73
DUKE
Not Isabel?
PROVOST   No.
DUKE   They will then, ere't be long.
PROVOST
What comfort is for Claudio?
DUKE
There's some in hope.
PROVOST   It is a bitter deputy.

---

65 *starkly* stiffly; *traveler* i.e., "travailler," laborer **66** *on* for **73** *curfew* bell
rung at night to signify that laws governing nighttime activities were in force

DUKE

   Not so, not so; his life is paralleled

78   Even with the stroke and line of his great justice.

   He doth with holy abstinence subdue

80   That in himself which he spurs on his power

81   To qualify in others. Were he mealed with that

   Which he corrects, then were he tyrannous,

   But this being so, he's just.

      [Knocking within.]   Now are they come.

                                 [Exit Provost.]

   This is a gentle provost; seldom when

85   The steelèd jailer is the friend of men.

      [Knocking.]

   How now, what noise? That spirit's possessed with haste

87   That wounds th' unsisting postern with these strokes.

      [Enter Provost.]

PROVOST

   There he must stay until the officer

89   Arise to let him in; he is called up.

DUKE

90   Have you no countermand for Claudio yet,

   But he must die tomorrow?

PROVOST   None, sir, none.

DUKE

   As near the dawning, provost, as it is,

93   You shall hear more ere morning.

PROVOST   Happily

   You something know, yet I believe there comes

95   No countermand; no such example have we.

96   Besides, upon the very siege of justice,

   Lord Angelo hath to the public ear

---

78 *the stroke and line of* i.e., the straight line followed by   81 *qualify* subdue; *mealed* stained   85 *steelèd* hardened   87 *unsisting* unresisting (?); *postern* side door   89 *called up* summoned   93 *Happily* perhaps   95 *example* precedent   96 *siege* seat

Professed the contrary.
Enter a Messenger.
DUKE
This is his lordship's man.
PROVOST
And here comes Claudio's pardon.   *100*
MESSENGER   My lord hath sent you this note, and by me
this further charge: that you swerve not from the small-
est article of it, neither in time, matter, or other circum-
stance. Good morrow, for, as I take it, it is almost day.
PROVOST   I shall obey him.   *[Exit Messenger.]*
DUKE   *[Aside]*
This is his pardon, purchased by such sin
For which the pardoner himself is in.   107
Hence hath offense his quick celerity,   108
When it is borne in high authority.   109
When vice makes mercy, mercy's so extended   *110*
That for the fault's love is th' offender friended.   111
Now, sir, what news?
PROVOST   I told you. Lord Angelo, belike thinking me
remiss in mine office, awakens me with this unwonted
putting on – methinks strangely, for he hath not used it   115
before.
DUKE   Pray you, let's hear.
[PROVOST]   *[Reads] the letter.* "Whatsoever you may hear
to the contrary, let Claudio be executed by four of the
clock, and, in the afternoon, Barnardine. For my better   *120*
satisfaction, let me have Claudio's head sent me by five.
Let this be duly performed, with a thought that more
depends on it than we must yet deliver. Thus fail not to   123
do your office, as you will answer it at your peril."
What say you to this, sir?

---

107 *For . . . in* i.e., of which the pardoner (Angelo) is guilty himself   108
quick celerity i.e., speedy vigor   109 *borne in* propelled by   111 *friended* be-
friended   115 *putting on* urging   123 *must . . . deliver* can yet make known

126 DUKE What is that Barnardine who is to be executed in
th' afternoon?

128 PROVOST A Bohemian born, but here nursed up and
129 bred; one that is a prisoner nine years old.

130 DUKE How came it that the absent duke had not either
delivered him to his liberty or executed him? I have
heard it was ever his manner to do so.

PROVOST His friends still wrought reprieves for him,
134 and, indeed, his fact, till now in the government of
Lord Angelo, came not to an undoubtful proof.

DUKE It is now apparent?

PROVOST Most manifest, and not denied by himself.

DUKE Hath he borne himself penitently in prison? How
139 seems he to be touched?

140 PROVOST A man that apprehends death no more dread-
fully but as a drunken sleep: careless, reckless, and fear-
less of what's past, present, or to come; insensible of
mortality, and desperately mortal.

144 DUKE He wants advice.

PROVOST He will hear none. He hath evermore had the
146 liberty of the prison; give him leave to escape hence, he
would not. Drunk many times a day, if not many days
entirely drunk. We have very oft awaked him, as if to
carry him to execution, and showed him a seeming
150 warrant for it; it hath not moved him at all.

151 DUKE More of him anon. There is written in your brow,
provost, honesty and constancy. If I read it not truly,
153 my ancient skill beguiles me; but in the boldness of my
154 cunning I will lay myself in hazard. Claudio, whom
155 here you have warrant to execute, is no greater forfeit to

---

126 *What* who 128 *nursed up* nurtured 129 *prisoner . . . old* i.e., he has
been a prisoner for nine years 134 *his fact* deed, crime 139 *touched* af-
fected 140 *apprehends* conceives 144 *wants* lacks 146 *liberty . . . prison*
free run of the prison 151 *More . . . anon* more about him in due course
153 *ancient skill* well-tried expertise 153–54 *boldness of my cunning* confi-
dence in my skill 154 *lay . . . hazard* take a gamble 155 *no greater forfeit*
no more in jeopardy

the law than Angelo who hath sentenced him. To make
you understand this in a manifested effect, I crave but   157
four days' respite, for the which you are to do me both
a present and a dangerous courtesy.

PROVOST   Pray, sir, in what?   160

DUKE   In the delaying death.

PROVOST   Alack, how may I do it, having the hour lim-   162
ited, and an express command, under penalty, to deliver his head in the view of Angelo? I may make my
case as Claudio's to cross this in the smallest.

DUKE   By the vow of mine order I warrant you. If my instructions may be your guide, let this Barnardine be
this morning executed, and his head borne to Angelo.

PROVOST   Angelo hath seen them both, and will discover   169
the favor.   170

DUKE   O, death's a great disguiser, and you may add to it.
Shave the head, and tie the beard, and say it was the desire of the penitent to be so bared before his death; you
know the course is common. If anything fall to you
upon this more than thanks and good fortune, by the
saint whom I profess, I will plead against it with my
life.

PROVOST   Pardon me, good father, it is against my oath.

DUKE   Were you sworn to the duke or to the deputy?

PROVOST   To him, and to his substitutes.   180

DUKE   You will think you have made no offense, if the
duke avouch the justice of your dealing?   182

PROVOST   But what likelihood is in that?

DUKE   Not a resemblance, but a certainty. Yet since I see
you fearful, that neither my coat, integrity, nor persuasion can with ease attempt you, I will go further than I   186
meant, to pluck all fears out of you. Look you, sir, here

---

157 *in . . . effect* by a revelation 162–63 *limited* stipulated 169–70 *dis-*
cover the favor recognize the face 182 *avouch* warrant 186 *attempt* persuade

188   is the hand and seal of the duke; you know the charac-
189   ter, I doubt not, and the signet is not strange to you.
190   PROVOST   I know them both.
      DUKE   The contents of this is the return of the duke. You
      shall anon overread it at your pleasure, where you shall
      find within these two days he will be here. This is a
      thing that Angelo knows not, for he this very day re-
      ceives letters of strange tenor, perchance of the duke's
      death, perchance entering into some monastery, but by
197   chance nothing of what is writ. Look, th' unfolding star
198   calls up the shepherd. Put not yourself into amazement
      how these things should be; all difficulties are but easy
200   when they are known. Call your executioner, and off
201   with Barnardine's head; I will give him a present shrift
      and advise him for a better place. Yet you are amazed,
      but this shall absolutely resolve you. Come away; it is
      almost clear dawn.   *Exit [with Provost].*
                              *

∾ **IV.3** *Enter Clown [Pompey].*

      POMPEY   I am as well acquainted here as I was in our
      house of profession. One would think it were Mistress
      Overdone's own house, for here be many of her old
      customers. First, here's young Master Rash; he's in for a
5   commodity of brown paper and old ginger, ninescore
6   and seventeen pounds, of which he made five marks
      ready money. Marry, then ginger was not much in re-
8   quest, for the old women were all dead. Then is there
      here one Master Caper, at the suit of Master Three-pile

188–89 *character* handwriting   189 *signet* seal   197 *nothing . . . writ* i.e., the
duke will do otherwise than what is written; *unfolding star* i.e., the morning
star, which tells the shepherd to release the sheep from the fold   198 *amazement* confusion   201 *present shrift* immediate confession and absolution
      IV.3 The prison   5 *a commodity* goods bought on credit for resale   6
marks coins valued at two thirds of a pound   8 *old women . . . dead* (old
women were believed to like *ginger*)

the mercer, for some four suits of peach-colored satin, 10
which now peaches him a beggar. Then have we here 11
young Dizzy, and young Master Deep-vow, and Master
Copper-spur, and Master Starve-lackey, the rapier and 13
dagger man, and young Drop-heir that killed lusty
Pudding, and Master Forthright the tilter, and brave 15
Master Shoe-tie the great traveler, and wild Half-can
that stabbed Pots, and I think forty more, all great
doers in our trade, and are now "for the Lord's sake." 18
    Enter Abhorson.

ABHORSON   Sirrah, bring Barnardine hither.

POMPEY   Master Barnardine, you must rise and be 20
hanged, Master Barnardine.

ABHORSON   What ho, Barnardine!

BARNARDINE   *[Within]* A pox o' your throats! Who
makes that noise there? What are you?

POMPEY   Your friends, sir, the hangman. You must be so
good, sir, to rise and be put to death.

BARNARDINE   *[Within]* Away, you rogue, away! I am
sleepy.

ABHORSON   Tell him he must awake, and that quickly
too. 30

POMPEY   Pray, Master Barnardine, awake till you are executed, and sleep afterwards.

ABHORSON   Go in to him, and fetch him out.

POMPEY   He is coming, sir, he is coming; I hear his straw
rustle.
    Enter Barnardine.

ABHORSON   Is the ax upon the block, sirrah?

POMPEY   Very ready, sir.

BARNARDINE   How now, Abhorson, what's the news with
you?

---

10 *mercer* dealer in fabrics 11 *peaches him* i.e., turns him in as **13–14**
rapier and dagger man fencer (who uses both these weapons) **15** *tilter*
fighter **18** *for the Lord's sake* (cry of poor prisoners through the grating, in
begging from passersby)

40 ABHORSON   Truly, sir, I would desire you to clap into
your prayers for, look you, the warrant's come.

BARNARDINE   You rogue, I have been drinking all night;
I am not fitted for't.

POMPEY   O, the better, sir, for he that drinks all night,
45 and is hanged betimes in the morning, may sleep the
sounder all the next day.
Enter Duke [disguised as before].

47 ABHORSON   Look you, sir, here comes your ghostly father. Do we jest now, think you?

DUKE   Sir, induced by my charity, and hearing how
50 hastily you are to depart, I am come to advise you,
comfort you, and pray with you.

BARNARDINE   Friar, not I. I have been drinking hard all
night and I will have more time to prepare me or they
54 shall beat out my brains with billets. I will not consent
to die this day, that's certain.

DUKE   O, sir, you must, and therefore I beseech you look
forward on the journey you shall go.

BARNARDINE   I swear I will not die today for any man's
persuasion.

60 DUKE   But hear you –

BARNARDINE   Not a word. If you have anything to say to
62 me, come to my ward, for thence will not I today. *Exit.*
Enter Provost.

DUKE
63 Unfit to live or die. O gravel heart!
After him, fellows, bring him to the block.
                              [Exeunt Abhorson and Pompey.]

PROVOST
Now, sir, how do you find the prisoner?

DUKE
66 A creature unprepared, unmeet for death,

---

40 *clap into* begin **45** *betimes* early **47–48** *ghostly father* i.e., spiritual father, confessor **54** *billets* cudgels **62** *ward* prison area **63** *gravel* stony
66 *unmeet* unfitting

And to transport him in the mind he is   67
Were damnable.
PROVOST   Here in the prison, father,
There died this morning of a cruel fever
One Ragozine, a most notorious pirate,   70
A man of Claudio's years, his beard and head
Just of his color. What if we do omit
This reprobate till he were well inclined,   73
And satisfy the deputy with the visage
Of Ragozine, more like to Claudio?
DUKE
O, 'tis an accident that heaven provides.
Dispatch it presently; the hour draws on   77
Prefixed by Angelo. See this be done,   78
And sent according to command, whiles I
Persuade this rude wretch willingly to die.   80
PROVOST
This shall be done, good father, presently.
But Barnardine must die this afternoon,
And how shall we continue Claudio,   83
To save me from the danger that might come
If he were known alive?
DUKE   Let this be done:
Put them in secret holds, both Barnardine and Claudio.   86
Ere twice the sun hath made his journal greeting   87
To yonder generation, you shall find
Your safety manifested.
PROVOST
I am your free dependent.   90
DUKE
Quick, dispatch, and send the head to Angelo.
                                        Exit [Provost].
Now will I write letters to Angelo –

---

67 *transport* dispatch   73 *reprobate* villain   77 *presently* at once   78 *Prefixed*
determined in advance   83 *continue* keep alive   86 *holds* cells   87 *journal*
daily   90 *your free dependent* freely at your service

The provost, he shall bear them – whose contents
Shall witness to him I am near at home,
95   And that by great injunctions I am bound
To enter publicly. Him I'll desire
97   To meet me at the consecrated fount
A league below the city, and from thence,
99   By cold gradation and well-balanced form,
100 We shall proceed with Angelo.
Enter Provost.

PROVOST
Here is the head. I'll carry it myself.

DUKE
Convenient is it. Make a swift return,
103 For I would commune with you of such things
104 That want no ear but yours.

PROVOST   I'll make all speed.   *Exit.*

ISABELLA   *[Within]*
Peace, ho, be here!

DUKE
The tongue of Isabel. She's come to know
If yet her brother's pardon be come hither,
But I will keep her ignorant of her good,
109 To make her heavenly comforts of despair
110 When it is least expected.
Enter Isabella.

ISABELLA   Ho, by your leave!

DUKE
Good morning to you, fair and gracious daughter.

ISABELLA
The better, given me by so holy a man.
Hath yet the deputy sent my brother's pardon?

---

95 *injunctions* (1) commands, (2) compelling necessities **97** *consecrated fount* holy spring **99** *cold gradation* unhurried progression; *well-balanced form* orderly process **103** *commune* talk **104** *want* require **109** *To . . . despair* i.e., turn despair into blessed happiness

DUKE
  He hath released him, Isabel, from the world.
  His head is off and sent to Angelo.
ISABELLA
  Nay, but it is not so.
DUKE
  It is no other. Show your wisdom, daughter,
  In your close patience.   118
ISABELLA
  O, I will to him and pluck out his eyes!
DUKE
  You shall not be admitted to his sight.   120
ISABELLA
  Unhappy Claudio, wretched Isabel,
  Injurious world, most damnèd Angelo!
DUKE
  This nor hurts him nor profits you a jot;
  Forbear it therefore, give your cause to heaven.
  Mark what I say, which you shall find
  By every syllable a faithful verity.
  The duke comes home tomorrow – nay, dry your eyes –
  One of our covent, and his confessor,   128
  Gives me this instance. Already he hath carried   129
  Notice to Escalus and Angelo,   130
  Who do prepare to meet him at the gates,
  There to give up their power. If you can, pace your wis-   132
    dom
  In that good path that I would wish it go,
  And you shall have your bosom on this wretch,   134
  Grace of the duke, revenges to your heart,
  And general honor.   136
ISABELLA   I am directed by you.

---

118 *close* silent   128 *covent* convent   129 *instance* proof   132 *pace* school
134 *bosom* desire   136 *am* will be

DUKE
    This letter then to Friar Peter give;
    'Tis that he sent me of the duke's return.
    Say, by this token, I desire his company
140   At Mariana's house tonight. Her cause and yours
141   I'll perfect him withal, and he shall bring you
    Before the duke; and to the head of Angelo
    Accuse him home and home. For my poor self,
144   I am combinèd by a sacred vow
    And shall be absent. Wend you with this letter;
    Command these fretting waters from your eyes
    With a light heart; trust not my holy order
148   If I pervert your course. Who's here?
        Enter Lucio.
LUCIO   Good even, friar, where's the provost?
150 DUKE   Not within, sir.
LUCIO   O pretty Isabella, I am pale at mine heart to see
152   thine eyes so red; thou must be patient. I am fain to
153   dine and sup with water and bran; I dare not for my
154   head fill my belly; one fruitful meal would set me to't.
   But they say the duke will be here tomorrow. By my
156   troth, Isabel, I loved thy brother. If the old fantastical
157   duke of dark corners had been at home, he had lived.
                   [Exit Isabella.]
158 DUKE   Sir, the duke is marvelous little beholding to your
   reports, but the best is, he lives not in them.
160 LUCIO   Friar, thou knowest not the duke so well as I do.
161   He's a better woodman than thou tak'st him for.
DUKE   Well, you'll answer this one day. Fare ye well.
LUCIO   Nay, tarry, I'll go along with thee; I can tell thee
   pretty tales of the duke.

---

141 *perfect* inform fully   144 *combinèd* bound   148 *pervert* deflect, distort
152 *am fain* am constrained   153–54 *for my head* for fear of losing my head
154 *one . . . to't* i.e., a single nourishing meal would be enough to revive my
sexual activity   156 *fantastical* bizarre, whimsical   157 *he had* he would
have   158 *beholding* in your debt   161 *woodman* hunter (here, of women)

DUKE   You have told me too many of him already, sir, if
they be true; if not true, none were enough.

LUCIO   I was once before him for getting a wench with
child.

DUKE   Did you such a thing?

LUCIO   Yes, marry, did I; but I was fain to forswear it.   170
They would else have married me to the rotten medlar.   171

DUKE   Sir, your company is fairer than honest. Rest you   172
well.

LUCIO   By my troth, I'll go with thee to the lane's end. If
bawdy talk offend you, we'll have very little of it. Nay,
friar, I am a kind of burr; I shall stick.   *Exeunt.*

                         ✳

∾ **IV.4** *Enter Angelo and Escalus.*

ESCALUS   Every letter he hath writ hath disvouched other.   1

ANGELO   In most uneven and distracted manner. His ac-   2
tions show much like to madness; pray heaven his wisdom be not tainted. And why meet him at the gates   4
and redeliver our authorities there?

ESCALUS   I guess not.

ANGELO   And why should we proclaim it, in an hour before his entering, that if any crave redress of injustice,
they should exhibit their petitions in the street?   9

ESCALUS   He shows his reason for that: to have a dispatch   10
of complaints, and to deliver us from devices hereafter,   11
which shall then have no power to stand against us.

ANGELO
Well, I beseech you let it be proclaimed.

---

170 *fain to forswear* obliged to deny   171 *medlar* fruit that must rot before it
can be enjoyed (metaphorically, women's genitals, here implicitly of a diseased prostitute)   172 *fairer* more appealing
    IV.4 Angelo's house   1 *disvouched* contradicted   2 *uneven* erratic   4
tainted diseased   9 *exhibit* present   10 *dispatch* quick settlement   11 *devices*
stratagems (legal recourses)

14   Betimes i' th' morn I'll call you at your house;
15   Give notice to such men of sort and suit
     As are to meet him.
ESCALUS   I shall, sir. Fare you well.
ANGELO   Good night.   *Exit [Escalus].*
18   This deed unshapes me quite, makes me unpregnant
     And dull to all proceedings. A deflowered maid,
20   And by an eminent body that enforced
     The law against it! But that her tender shame
     Will not proclaim against her maiden loss,
23   How might she tongue me! Yet reason dares her no,
24   For my authority bears off a credent bulk,
     That no particular scandal once can touch
26   But it confounds the breather. He should have lived,
27   Save that his riotous youth with dangerous sense
28   Might in the times to come have ta'en revenge,
     By so receiving a dishonored life
30   With ransom of such shame. Would yet he had lived.
     Alack, when once our grace we have forgot,
32   Nothing goes right; we would, and we would not. *Exit.*

                           *

∾ IV.5   *Enter Duke [in his own habit] and Friar Peter.*

DUKE
     These letters at fit time deliver me.
     The provost knows our purpose and our plot.
3   The matter being afoot, keep your instruction,

---

14 *Betimes* early   15 *sort and suit* high rank and retinue   18 *unshapes* undoes; *unpregnant* at a loss   20 *eminent body* highly placed official   23 *tongue* accuse; *reason . . . no* i.e., reason will tell her she dare not   24 *bears . . . bulk* i.e., repels or overbears much that might otherwise be credited   26 *But . . . confounds* without confounding; *breather* i.e., the accuser   27 *sense* inclinations   28–30 *Might . . . shame* (either "might have taken revenge by repeating the crime" or "might have taken revenge on me for the shame of his deliverance")   32 *we . . . not* i.e., we do and don't want to do the things we do
IV.5 Near Vienna   3 *keep your instruction* stick to your orders

And hold you ever to our special drift,   4
Though sometimes you do blench from this to that,   5
As cause doth minister. Go call at Flavius' house,   6
And tell him where I stay; give the like notice
To Valencius, Rowland, and to Crassus,
And bid them bring the trumpets to the gate,   9
But send me Flavius first.   10
FRIAR PETER   It shall be speeded well.
                                              [Exit.]

    Enter Varrius.

DUKE
I thank thee, Varrius; thou hast made good haste.
Come, we will walk; there's other of our friends
Will greet us here anon, my gentle Varrius.   *Exeunt.*
                         *

∾ **IV.6** *Enter Isabella and Mariana.*

ISABELLA
To speak so indirectly I am loath.   1
I would say the truth, but to accuse him so,
That is your part. Yet I am advised to do it,
He says, to veil full purpose.
MARIANA   Be ruled by him.
ISABELLA
Besides, he tells me that if peradventure   5
He speak against me on the adverse side,
I should not think it strange, for 'tis a physic   7
That's bitter to sweet end.
MARIANA
I would Friar Peter –
    Enter [Friar] Peter.

---

4 *drift* aim 5 *blench . . . that* i.e., make tactical adjustments 6 *cause doth minister* necessity dictates 9 *trumpets* trumpeters 10 *speeded well* efficiently performed
    IV.6 A street in Vienna 1 *indirectly* deviously 5 *peradventure* perhaps 7 *physic* medicine

ISABELLA   O, peace, the friar is come.
FRIAR PETER
10   Come, I have found you out a stand most fit,
     Where you may have such vantage on the duke
     He shall not pass you. Twice have the trumpets sounded.
13   The generous and gravest citizens
14   Have hent the gates, and very near upon
     The duke is ent'ring; therefore hence, away.   *Exeunt.*

                          *

❧ **V.1** *Enter Duke, Varrius, Lords, Angelo, Escalus,
   Lucio, [Provost, Officers, and] Citizens at several
   doors.*

DUKE
1   My very worthy cousin, fairly met.
     Our old and faithful friend, we are glad to see you.
ANGELO, ESCALUS
     Happy return be to your royal grace.
DUKE
     Many and hearty thankings to you both.
5   We have made inquiry of you, and we hear
     Such goodness of your justice that our soul
     Cannot but yield you forth to public thanks,
8   Forerunning more requital.
ANGELO   You make my bonds still
       greater.
DUKE
     O, your desert speaks loud, and I should wrong it
10   To lock it in the wards of covert bosom,
11   When it deserves with characters of brass

---

10 *stand* place to stand   13 *generous* wellborn   14 *hent* placed themselves at;
very near upon almost at once

   V.1 The city gates   1 *cousin* (courteous form of address by a ruler to a nobleman)   5 *made inquiry . . . you* inquired into your doings   8 *Forerunning . . . requital* preceding further reward   10 *wards . . . bosom* i.e., hidden
recesses of my breast   11 *characters* letters

A forted residence 'gainst the tooth of time   12
And razure of oblivion. Give me your hand,   13
And let the subject see, to make them know
That outward courtesies would fain proclaim   15
Favors that keep within. Come, Escalus,   16
You must walk by us on our other hand,
And good supporters are you.
  Enter [Friar] Peter and Isabella.

FRIAR PETER
Now is your time. Speak loud and kneel before him.

ISABELLA
Justice, O royal duke! Vail your regard   20
Upon a wronged – I would fain have said, a maid.
O worthy prince, dishonor not your eye
By throwing it on any other object
Till you have heard me in my true complaint
And given me justice, justice, justice, justice!

DUKE
Relate your wrongs. In what? By whom? Be brief.
Here is Lord Angelo shall give you justice;
Reveal yourself to him.   28

ISABELLA   O worthy duke,
You bid me seek redemption of the devil.
Hear me yourself, for that which I must speak   *30*
Must either punish me, not being believed,   *31*
Or wring redress from you. Hear me, O hear me, here!

ANGELO
My lord, her wits, I fear me, are not firm.
She hath been a suitor to me for her brother,
Cut off by course of justice –

ISABELLA
By course of justice!

---

12 *forted* fortified   13 *razure* erasure   15 *would fain proclaim* i.e., are meant
to signify   16 *Favors . . . within* good intents that remain concealed   20
Vail your regard cast down your look   28 *Reveal* explain   31 *punish me* result
in my punishment

ANGELO
  And she will speak most bitterly and strange.
ISABELLA
  Most strange, but yet most truly, will I speak.
  That Angelo's forsworn, is it not strange?
40 That Angelo's a murderer, is't not strange?
41 That Angelo is an adulterous thief,
  An hypocrite, a virgin-violator,
  Is it not strange, and strange?
DUKE   Nay, it is ten times strange.
ISABELLA
  It is not truer he is Angelo
  Than this is all as true as it is strange.
  Nay, it is ten times true, for truth is truth
  To th' end of reck'ning.
DUKE   Away with her. Poor soul,
48 She speaks this in th' infirmity of sense.
ISABELLA
  O prince, I conjure thee, as thou believ'st
50 There is another comfort than this world,
51 That thou neglect me not with that opinion
  That I am touched with madness. Make not impossible
  That which but seems unlike. 'Tis not impossible
54 But one, the wicked'st caitiff on the ground,
  May seem as shy, as grave, as just, as absolute
  As Angelo. Even so may Angelo,
57 In all his dressings, caracts, titles, forms,
  Be an arch-villain. Believe it, royal prince.
  If he be less, he's nothing; but he's more,
60 Had I more name for badness.
DUKE   By mine honesty,
  If she be mad, as I believe no other,

---

41 *adulterous thief* i.e., thief of women's virginity   **48** *infirmity of sense* mental derangement   **51** *neglect . . . with* ignore me because of   **54** *caitiff* wretch   **57** *caracts* insignia of office

Her madness hath the oddest frame of sense,   62
Such a dependency of thing on thing,   63
As e'er I heard in madness.
ISABELLA   O gracious duke,
Harp not on that, nor do not banish reason
For inequality, but let your reason serve   66
To make the truth appear where it seems hid,
And hide the false seems true.   68
DUKE   Many that are not mad
Have sure more lack of reason. What would you say?   69
ISABELLA
I am the sister of one Claudio,   70
Condemned upon the act of fornication
To lose his head, condemned by Angelo.
I, in probation of a sisterhood,   73
Was sent to by my brother, one Lucio
As then the messenger –
LUCIO   That's I, an't like your grace.
I came to her from Claudio, and desired her
To try her gracious fortune with Lord Angelo
For her poor brother's pardon.
ISABELLA   That's he indeed.
DUKE
You were not bid to speak.
LUCIO   No, my good lord,
Nor wished to hold my peace.   80
DUKE   I wish you now, then.
Pray you, take note of it, and when you have
A business for yourself, pray heaven you then
Be perfect.   83
LUCIO   I warrant your honor.

---

62 *frame of sense* rational consistency   63 *dependency* logical connection   **66**
inequality (1) unequal status, (2) apparent deviation from the established
view (?)   68 *seems* that seems   69 *would you* do you wish to   73 *in proba-*
tion a novice   83 *perfect* well prepared

DUKE
  The warrant's for yourself: take heed to't.
ISABELLA
  This gentleman told somewhat of my tale –
LUCIO   Right.
DUKE
  It may be right, but you are i' the wrong
  To speak before your time. Proceed.
ISABELLA   I went
  To this pernicious caitiff deputy –
DUKE
90   That's somewhat madly spoken.
ISABELLA   Pardon it,
91   The phrase is to the matter.
DUKE
  Mended again. The matter: proceed.
ISABELLA
  In brief, to set the needless process by –
  How I persuaded, how I prayed, and kneeled,
95   How he refelled me, and how I replied,
  For this was of much length – the vile conclusion
  I now begin with grief and shame to utter.
  He would not, but by gift of my chaste body
99   To his concupiscible intemperate lust,
100   Release my brother; and after much debatement
101   My sisterly remorse confutes mine honor,
  And I did yield to him; but the next morn betimes,
103   His purpose surfeiting, he sends a warrant
  For my poor brother's head.
DUKE   This is most likely!
ISABELLA
  O, that it were as like as it is true.

---

91 *matter* purpose   95 *refelled* rebuffed   99 *concupiscible* desire-inflamed
101 *remorse* pity   103 *surfeiting* being sexually satiated

DUKE

By heaven, fond wretch, thou know'st not what thou
   speak'st,
Or else thou art suborned against his honor
In hateful practice. First, his integrity   108
Stands without blemish. Next, it imports no reason   109
That with such vehemency he should pursue   110
Faults proper to himself. If he had so offended,   111
He would have weighed thy brother by himself,
And not have cut him off. Someone hath set you on.
Confess the truth, and say by whose advice
Thou cam'st here to complain.

ISABELLA   And is this all?
Then, O you blessèd ministers above,   116
Keep me in patience, and with ripened time
Unfold the evil which is here wrapped up
In countenance. Heaven shield your grace from woe,   119
As I thus wronged hence unbelievèd go.   *120*

DUKE

I know you'd fain be gone. An officer!
To prison with her. Shall we thus permit
A blasting and a scandalous breath to fall   123
On him so near us? This needs must be a practice.   124
Who knew of your intent and coming hither?

ISABELLA

One that I would were here, Friar Lodowick.

DUKE

A ghostly father, belike. Who knows that Lodowick?

LUCIO

My lord, I know him; 'tis a meddling friar,
I do not like the man. Had he been lay, my lord,   129

---

108 *practice* conspiracy   **109** *imports no reason* makes no sense   **110** *pursue*
hunt down   **111** *proper to himself* of his own   **116** *ministers* angels   **119** *In
countenance* under protection of authority and good appearances   **123** *blasting* blighting   **124** *practice* plot   **129** *lay* i.e., a layman

130   For certain words he spake against your grace
131   In your retirement I had swinged him soundly.
DUKE
132   Words against me? This' a good friar, belike,
      And to set on this wretched woman here
      Against our substitute! Let this friar be found.
LUCIO
      But yesternight, my lord, she and that friar,
136   I saw them at the prison; a saucy friar,
137   A very scurvy fellow.
FRIAR PETER
      Blessèd be your royal grace!
      I have stood by, my lord, and I have heard
140   Your royal ear abused. First, hath this woman
      Most wrongfully accused your substitute,
      Who is as free from touch or soil with her
143   As she from one ungot.
DUKE   We did believe no less.
      Know you that Friar Lodowick that she speaks of?
FRIAR PETER
      I know him for a man divine and holy,
146   Not scurvy, nor a temporary meddler,
      As he's reported by this gentleman;
      And, on my trust, a man that never yet
      Did, as he vouches, misreport your grace.
LUCIO
150   My lord, most villainously, believe it.
FRIAR PETER
      Well, he in time may come to clear himself,
      But at this instant he is sick, my lord,
153   Of a strange fever. Upon his mere request,
      Being come to knowledge that there was complaint
      Intended 'gainst Lord Angelo, came I hither,

---

131 *swinged* beaten   132 *This'* this is   136 *saucy* impertinent   137 *scurvy*
worthless   143 *ungot* not yet born   146 *temporary* temporal   153 *mere* sole
and personal

To speak, as from his mouth, what he doth know
Is true and false, and what he with his oath
And all probation will make up full clear,   158
Whensoever he's convented. First, for this woman,   159
To justify this worthy nobleman,   160
So vulgarly and personally accused,
Her shall you hear disprovèd to her eyes,
Till she herself confess it.
DUKE   Good friar, let's hear it.
    [Isabella withdraws, guarded.]
    Enter Mariana.
Do you not smile at this, Lord Angelo?
O heaven, the vanity of wretched fools!
Give us some seats. Come, cousin Angelo,
In this I'll be impartial; be you judge   167
Of your own cause. Is this the witness, friar?
First, let her show her face, and after speak.
MARIANA
Pardon, my lord, I will not show my face   170
Until my husband bid me.
DUKE   What, are you married?
MARIANA   No, my lord.
DUKE   Are you a maid?
MARIANA   No, my lord.
DUKE   A widow, then?
MARIANA   Neither, my lord.
DUKE   Why, you are nothing then; neither maid, widow,
    nor wife?
LUCIO   My lord, she may be a punk, for many of them   180
    are neither maid, widow, nor wife.
DUKE
    Silence that fellow. I would he had some cause
    To prattle for himself.
LUCIO   Well, my lord.

---

158 *probation* proof   **159** *convented* summoned   **167** *impartial* nonpartici-
pant   **180** *punk* prostitute

MARIANA
   My lord, I do confess I ne'er was married,
   And I confess besides I am no maid.
187   I have known my husband, yet my husband
   Knows not that ever he knew me.
LUCIO   He was drunk, then, my lord; it can be no better.
190 DUKE   For the benefit of silence, would thou wert so too.
LUCIO   Well, my lord.
DUKE
   This is no witness for Lord Angelo.
MARIANA
   Now I come to't, my lord.
   She that accuses him of fornication,
   In selfsame manner doth accuse my husband,
196 And charges him, my lord, with such a time
   When, I'll depose, I had him in mine arms,
198 With all th' effect of love.
ANGELO
   Charges she more than me?
MARIANA   Not that I know.
DUKE
200 No? You say your husband?
MARIANA
   Why, just, my lord, and that is Angelo,
   Who thinks he knows that he ne'er knew my body,
   But knows, he thinks, that he knows Isabel's.
ANGELO
204 This is a strange abuse. Let's see thy face.
MARIANA
   My husband bids me; now I will unmask.
     [Unveiling]
   This is that face, thou cruel Angelo,
   Which once thou swor'st was worth the looking on.
208 This is the hand which, with a vowed contract,

---

187 *known* had sex with   196 *with* at   198 *th' effect* the manifestations
204 *abuse* deception   208 *vowed contract* formal betrothal

Was fast belocked in thine. This is the body
That took away the match from Isabel,   *210*
And did supply thee at thy garden house   211
In her imagined person.
DUKE   Know you this woman?
LUCIO
Carnally, she says.
DUKE   Sirrah, no more!
LUCIO
Enough, my lord.
ANGELO
My lord, I must confess I know this woman,
And five years since there was some speech of marriage
Betwixt myself and her, which was broke off,
Partly for that her promisèd proportions   218
Came short of composition, but in chief   219
For that her reputation was disvalued   220
In levity; since which time of five years   221
I never spake with her, saw her, nor heard from her,
Upon my faith and honor.
MARIANA   Noble prince,
As there comes light from heaven and words from
    breath,
As there is sense in truth and truth in virtue,
I am affianced this man's wife as strongly   226
As words could make up vows; and, my good lord,
But Tuesday night last gone in's garden house
He knew me as a wife. As this is true,
Let me in safety raise me from my knees   *230*
Or else forever be confixèd here   231
A marble monument.
ANGELO   I did but smile till now.
Now, good my lord, give me the scope of justice;   233

---

211 *supply* gratify **218** *proportions* dowry **219** *composition* what had been
agreed upon **220** *disvalued* discredited **221** *In levity* for lightness **226** *affianced* betrothed **231** *confixèd* fixed in place **233** *scope* full powers

My patience here is touched. I do perceive
235   These poor informal women are no more
236   But instruments of some more mightier member
That sets them on. Let me have way, my lord,
To find this practice out.

DUKE   Ay, with my heart,
And punish them to your height of pleasure.
240   Thou foolish friar, and thou pernicious woman,
241   Compact with her that's gone, think'st thou thy oaths,
Though they would swear down each particular saint,
Were testimonies against his worth and credit
244   That's sealed in approbation? You, Lord Escalus,
Sit with my cousin; lend him your kind pains
To find out this abuse, whence 'tis derived.
There is another friar that set them on;
Let him be sent for.

FRIAR PETER
Would he were here, my lord, for he indeed
250   Hath set the women on to this complaint.
Your provost knows the place where he abides
And he may fetch him.

DUKE   Go do it instantly.
[Exit Provost.]
253   And you, my noble and well-warranted cousin,
Whom it concerns to hear this matter forth,
Do with your injuries as seems you best,
In any chastisement. I for a while
Will leave you, but stir not you till you have
258   Well determined upon these slanderers.

ESCALUS
259   My lord, we'll do it throughly.   *Exit [Duke].*

---

235 *informal* disorderly 236 *member* person 241 *Compact with* in league
with 244 *That's sealed in approbation* that carries (my) seal of approval
253 *well-warranted* fully sanctioned and approved 258 *Well determined*
passed well-founded judgment 259 *throughly* thoroughly

Signor Lucio, did not you say you knew that Friar   *260*
Lodowick to be a dishonest person?

LUCIO   *Cucullus non facit monachum;* honest in nothing   *262*
but in his clothes, and one that hath spoke most villainous speeches of the duke.

ESCALUS   We shall entreat you to abide here till he come
and enforce them against him. We shall find this friar a   *266*
notable fellow.

LUCIO   As any in Vienna, on my word.

ESCALUS   Call that same Isabel here once again; I would
speak with her. *[Exit an Attendant.]* Pray you, my lord,   *270*
give me leave to question; you shall see how I'll handle
her.

LUCIO   Not better than he, by her own report.

ESCALUS   Say you?

LUCIO   Marry, sir, I think, if you handled her privately,
she would sooner confess; perchance publicly she'll be
ashamed.

   Enter Duke [in his friar's habit], Provost, Isabella
   [, and Officers].

ESCALUS   I will go darkly to work with her.   *278*

LUCIO   That's the way, for women are light at midnight.

ESCALUS   Come on, mistress, here's a gentlewoman de-   *280*
nies all that you have said.

LUCIO   My lord, here comes the rascal I spoke of – here
with the provost.

ESCALUS   In very good time. Speak not you to him, till
we call upon you.

LUCIO   Mum.

ESCALUS   Come, sir, did you set these women on to slander Lord Angelo? They have confessed you did.

DUKE   'Tis false.

ESCALUS   How! Know you where you are?   *290*

---

262 *Cucullus . . . monachum* a cowl doesn't make a monk   **266** *enforce* bring
in evidence   **278** *darkly* craftily

DUKE

 Respect to your great place, and let the devil

292 Be sometime honored for his burning throne.

 Where is the duke? 'Tis he should hear me speak.

ESCALUS

 The duke's in us, and we will hear you speak.

295 Look you speak justly.

DUKE

 Boldly at least. But O, poor souls,

 Come you to seek the lamb here of the fox?

 Good night to your redress! Is the duke gone?

 Then is your cause gone too. The duke's unjust,

300 Thus to retort your manifest appeal

 And put your trial in the villain's mouth

 Which here you come to accuse.

LUCIO

 This is the rascal; this is he I spoke of.

ESCALUS

 Why, thou unreverend and unhallowed friar,

 Is't not enough thou hast suborned these women

 To accuse this worthy man but, in foul mouth,

307 And in the witness of his proper ear,

308 To call him villain? And then to glance from him

309 To th' duke himself, to tax him with injustice?

310 Take him hence; to th' rack with him. We'll touse you

 Joint by joint, but we will know his purpose.

 What, unjust?

DUKE   Be not so hot. The duke

 Dare no more stretch this finger of mine than he

 Dare rack his own. His subject am I not,

315 Nor here provincial. My business in this state

 Made me a looker-on here in Vienna,

---

292 *sometime* on occasion 295 *justly* truthfully 300 *retort* turn back; *manifest* plainly true 307 *the witness . . . ear* i.e., in his own hearing 308 *glance* deflect (your accusation) 309 *tax* accuse 310 *touse* tear 315 *provincial* i.e., under the jurisdiction of this province

Where I have seen corruption boil and bubble
Till it o'errun the stew. Laws for all faults,   318
But faults so countenanced that the strong statutes
Stand like the forfeits in a barber's shop,   320
As much in mock as mark.

ESCALUS
Slander to th' state. Away with him to prison.

ANGELO
What can you vouch against him, Signor Lucio?   323
Is this the man that you did tell us of?

LUCIO 'Tis he, my lord. Come hither, goodman bald-   325
pate. Do you know me?

DUKE I remember you, sir, by the sound of your voice. I
met you at the prison in the absence of the duke.

LUCIO O, did you so? And do you remember what you
said of the duke?   330

DUKE Most notedly, sir.   331

LUCIO Do you so, sir? And was the duke a fleshmonger,   332
a fool, and a coward, as you then reported him to be?

DUKE You must, sir, change persons with me, ere you
make that my report. You, indeed, spoke so of him, and
much more, much worse.

LUCIO O thou damnable fellow, did not I pluck thee by
the nose for thy speeches?

DUKE I protest I love the duke as I love myself.

ANGELO Hark how the villain would close now, after his   340
treasonable abuses.

ESCALUS Such a fellow is not to be talked withal; away   342
with him to prison. Where is the provost? Away with
him to prison, lay bolts enough upon him, let him   344
speak no more. Away with those giglets too, and with   345
the other confederate companion.

---

318 *stew* boiling pot (also punning on *stew* as brothel) **320** *forfeits . . . shop*
i.e., trivial rules of the kind imposed in barbershops **323** *vouch* give in evidence **325–26** *baldpate* i.e., monk with a shaven head **331** *notedly* precisely **332** *fleshmonger* pimp **340** *close* i.e., come to a good conclusion
342 *withal* with **344** *bolts* fetters **345** *giglets* immoral women

[The Provost lays hands on the Duke.]

DUKE   Stay, sir, stay a while.

ANGELO   What, resists he? Help him, Lucio.

LUCIO   Come, sir, come, sir, come, sir. Foh, sir, why, you
350   bald-pated, lying rascal, you must be hooded, must
you? Show your knave's visage, with a pox to you; show
352   your sheep-biting face, and be hanged an hour. Will't
not off?

[Pulls off the friar's hood, and discovers the Duke.]

DUKE

Thou art the first knave that e'er mad'st a duke.

First, provost, let me bail these gentle three –

[To Lucio]

Sneak not away, sir, for the friar and you

Must have a word anon. Lay hold on him.

LUCIO

This may prove worse than hanging.

DUKE   *[To Escalus]*

What you have spoke I pardon. Sit you down,

360   We'll borrow place of him. *[To Angelo]* Sir, by your leave.

361   Hast thou or word or wit or impudence

362   That yet can do thee office? If thou hast,

Rely upon it till my tale be heard,

364   And hold no longer out.

ANGELO   O my dread lord,

I should be guiltier than my guiltiness

To think I can be undiscernible,

When I perceive your grace, like power divine,

368   Hath looked upon my passes. Then, good prince,

No longer session hold upon my shame,

370   But let my trial be mine own confession.

371   Immediate sentence, then, and sequent death

---

352 *sheep-biting* villainous (from dogs that bite sheep); *an hour* within the
hour 361 *or ... or ... or* either ... or ... or 362 *do thee office* do you
service 364 *hold ... out* admit the truth at once 368 *passes* deeds 371 *sequent* consequent

Is all the grace I beg.
DUKE   Come hither, Mariana.
Say, wast thou ere contracted to this woman?
ANGELO
I was, my lord.
DUKE
Go take her hence, and marry her instantly.
Do you the office, friar; which consummate,   376
Return him here again. Go with him, provost.
                    Exeunt [Angelo, with Mariana,
                         Friar Peter, and Provost].

ESCALUS
My lord, I am more amazed at his dishonor
Than at the strangeness of it.
DUKE   Come hither, Isabel.
Your friar is now your prince. As I was then   380
Advertising and holy to your business,   381
Not changing heart with habit, I am still
Attorneyed at your service.   383
ISABELLA   O, give me pardon,
That I, your vassal, have employed and pained   384
Your unknown sovereignty.
DUKE   You are pardoned, Isabel;
And now, dear maid, be you as free to us.   386
Your brother's death, I know, sits at your heart,
And you may marvel why I obscured myself,
Laboring to save his life, and would not rather
Make rash remonstrance of my hidden power   390
Than let him so be lost. O most kind maid,
It was the swift celerity of his death,
Which I did think with slower foot came on,
That brained my purpose; but peace be with him.   394
That life is better life past fearing death,

---

376 *consummate* concluded 381 *Advertising* attentive; *holy* honestly devoted 383 *Attorneyed* acting for you 384 *vassal* subject 386 *free* generous 390 *rash remonstrance* blatant demonstration 394 *brained* killed

Than that which lives to fear. Make it your comfort,
So happy is your brother.

    Enter Angelo, Mariana, [Friar] Peter, Provost.

ISABELLA   I do, my lord.

DUKE

For this new-married man approaching here,

399   Whose salt imagination yet hath wronged

400   Your well-defended honor, you must pardon
For Mariana's sake. But as he adjudged your brother,
Being criminal, in double violation
Of sacred chastity, and of promise breach,
Thereon dependent, for your brother's life,
The very mercy of the law cries out

406   Most audible, even from his proper tongue,
"An Angelo for Claudio, death for death!
Haste still pays haste, and leisure answers leisure,
Like doth quit like, and Measure still for Measure."

410   Then, Angelo, thy fault's thus manifested,

411   Which though thou wouldst deny, denies thee vantage.
We do condemn thee to the very block
Where Claudio stooped to death, and with like haste.
Away with him.

MARIANA   O, my most gracious lord,
I hope you will not mock me with a husband.

DUKE

It is your husband mocked you with a husband.
Consenting to the safeguard of your honor,
I thought your marriage fit; else imputation,
For that he knew you, might reproach your life

420   And choke your good to come. For his possessions,
Although by confiscation they are ours,
We do instate and widow you with all,
To buy you a better husband.

MARIANA   O my dear lord,
I crave no other, nor no better man.

---

399 *salt* lecherous   **406** *proper* very own   **411** *vantage* a way out

DUKE
  Never crave him; we are definitive.
MARIANA
  Gentle my liege –
DUKE   You do but lose your labor.
  Away with him to death. *[To Lucio]* Now, sir, to you.
MARIANA
  O my good lord! Sweet Isabel, take my part,
  Lend me your knees, and, all my life to come,
  I'll lend you all my life to do you service.   430
DUKE
  Against all sense you do importune her.   431
  Should she kneel down in mercy of this fact,   432
  Her brother's ghost his pavèd bed would break,   433
  And take her hence in horror.
MARIANA   Isabel,
  Sweet Isabel, do yet but kneel by me,
  Hold up your hands, say nothing, I'll speak all.
  They say best men are molded out of faults,
  And, for the most, become much more the better
  For being a little bad; so may my husband.
  O Isabel, will you not lend a knee?   440
DUKE
  He dies for Claudio's death.
ISABELLA   *[Kneeling]*   Most bounteous sir,
  Look, if it please you, on this man condemned
  As if my brother lived. I partly think
  A due sincerity governed his deeds
  Till he did look on me. Since it is so,
  Let him not die; my brother had but justice,
  In that he did the thing for which he died.
  For Angelo,
  His act did not o'ertake his bad intent,   449
  And must be buried but as an intent   450

---

431 *sense* reason   **432** *fact* crime   **433** *pavèd* covered with slabs   **449** *o'ertake* succeed

451   That perished by the way. Thoughts are no subjects,
Intents but merely thoughts.

MARIANA   Merely, my lord.

DUKE

453   Your suit's unprofitable; stand up, I say.
I have bethought me of another fault.
Provost, how came it Claudio was beheaded
At an unusual hour?

PROVOST   It was commanded so.

DUKE

Had you a special warrant for the deed?

PROVOST

No, my good lord, it was by private message.

DUKE

For which I do discharge you of your office;
460   Give up your keys.

PROVOST   Pardon me, noble lord;
461   I thought it was a fault, but knew it not,
462   Yet did repent me after more advice;
For testimony whereof, one in the prison
That should by private order else have died
I have reserved alive.

DUKE   What's he?

PROVOST   His name is Barnardine.

DUKE

I would thou hadst done so by Claudio.
Go, fetch him hither; let me look upon him.

                                [Exit Provost.]

ESCALUS

I am sorry, one so learned and so wise
469   As you, Lord Angelo, have still appeared,
470   Should slip so grossly, both in the heat of blood
And lack of tempered judgment afterward.

---

451 *Thoughts . . . subjects* i.e., thoughts are not liable to prosecution   **453** *unprofitable* without merit   **461** *knew it not* wasn't certain   **462** *more advice* further reflection   **469** *still* always

ANGELO

   I am sorry that such sorrow I procure,   472

   And so deep sticks it in my penitent heart

   That I crave death more willingly than mercy;

   'Tis my deserving, and I do entreat it.

     Enter Barnardine and Provost, Claudio [muffled],

     Juliet.

DUKE

   Which is that Barnardine?

PROVOST   This, my lord.

DUKE

   There was a friar told me of this man.

   Sirrah, thou art said to have a stubborn soul,

   That apprehends no further than this world,   479

   And squar'st thy life according. Thou'rt condemned,   480

   But, for those earthly faults, I quit them all,   481

   And pray thee take this mercy to provide

   For better times to come. Friar, advise him;

   I leave him to your hand. What muffled fellow's that?

PROVOST

   This is another prisoner that I saved,

   Who should have died when Claudio lost his head,

   As like almost to Claudio as himself.

     [Unmuffles Claudio.]

DUKE   *[To Isabella]*

   If he be like your brother, for his sake

   Is he pardoned, and for your lovely sake.

   Give me your hand and say you will be mine;   *490*

   He is my brother too. But fitter time for that.

   By this Lord Angelo perceives he's safe;

   Methinks I see a quick'ning in his eye.

   Well, Angelo, your evil quits you well.   494

   Look that you love your wife, her worth, worth yours.   495

---

472 *procure* cause 479 *apprehends* envisions 480 *squar'st* regulate 481
quit pardon 494 *quits* requites 495 *worth . . . yours* her worth equals yours

496 I find an apt remission in myself,
497 And yet here's one in place I cannot pardon.
    [To Lucio]
    You, sirrah, that knew me for a fool, a coward,
499 One all of luxury, an ass, a madman,
500 Wherein have I so deserved of you,
    That you extol me thus?

LUCIO 'Faith, my lord, I spoke it but according to the
503 trick. If you will hang me for it, you may, but I had
    rather it would please you, I might be whipped.

DUKE
    Whipped first, sir, and hanged after.
    Proclaim it, provost, round about the city,
    If any woman wronged by this lewd fellow –
    As I have heard him swear himself there's one
    Whom he begot with child – let her appear,
510 And he shall marry her. The nuptial finished,
    Let him be whipped and hanged.

LUCIO I beseech your highness, do not marry me to a
    whore. Your highness said even now, I made you a
    duke; good my lord, do not recompense me in making
    me a cuckold.

DUKE
    Upon mine honor, thou shalt marry her.
    Thy slanders I forgive, and therewithal
518 Remit thy other forfeits. Take him to prison,
    And see our pleasure herein executed.

520 LUCIO Marrying a punk, my lord, is pressing to death,
    whipping, and hanging.

DUKE
    Slandering a prince deserves it.
                        [Exeunt Officers with Lucio.]

---

496 *apt remission* ready forgiveness 497 *in place* here 499 *luxury* lechery
503 *trick* fashion 518 *Remit ... forfeits* waive your other penalties 520
pressing ... death torture in which victims are pressed under progressively
heavier weights until they are crushed

She, Claudio, that you wronged, look you restore.
Joy to you, Mariana; love her, Angelo;
I have confessed her and I know her virtue.
Thanks, good friend Escalus, for thy much goodness;
There's more behind that is more gratulate.   527
Thanks, provost, for thy care and secrecy;
We shall employ thee in a worthier place.
Forgive him, Angelo, that brought you home   530
The head of Ragozine for Claudio's;
Th' offense pardons itself. Dear Isabel,
I have a motion much imports your good,   533
Whereto if you'll a willing ear incline,
What's mine is yours, and what is yours is mine.
So, bring us to our palace, where we'll show
What's yet behind, that's meet you all should know.   537

[Exeunt.]

---

527 *gratulate* gratifying 533 *motion* proposition 537 *yet behind* yet to come; *meet* proper

The distinguished Pelican Shakespeare series, newly revised
to be the premier choice for students, professors, and
general readers well into the 21st century

All's Well That Ends Well
ISBN 0-14-071460-X

Antony and Cleopatra
ISBN 0-14-071452-9

As You Like It
ISBN 0-14-071471-5

The Comedy of Errors
ISBN 0-14-071474-X

Coriolanus
ISBN 0-14-071473-1

Cymbeline
ISBN 0-14-071472-3

Hamlet
ISBN 0-14-071454-5

Henry IV, Part I
ISBN 0-14-071456-1

Henry IV, Part 2
ISBN 0-14-071457-X

Henry V
ISBN 0-14-071458-8

Henry VI, Part 1
ISBN 0-14-071465-0

Henry VI, Part 2
ISBN 0-14-071466-9

Henry VI, Part 3
ISBN 0-14-071467-7

Henry VIII
ISBN 0-14-071475-8

Julius Caesar
ISBN 0-14-071468-5

King John
ISBN 0-14-071459-6

King Lear
ISBN 0-14-071476-6

King Lear (The Quarto and Folio Texts)
ISBN 0-14-071490-1

Love's Labor's Lost
ISBN 0-14-071477-4

Macbeth
ISBN 0-14-071478-2

Measure for Measure
ISBN 0-14-071479-0

The Merchant of Venice
ISBN 0-14-071462-6

The Merry Wives of Windsor
ISBN 0-14-071464-2

A Midsummer Night's Dream
ISBN 0-14-071455-3

Much Ado About Nothing
ISBN 0-14-071480-4

The Narrative Poems
ISBN 0-14-071481-2

Othello
ISBN 0-14-071463-4

Pericles
ISBN 0-14-071469-3

Richard II
ISBN 0-14-071482-0

Richard III
ISBN 0-14-071483-9

Romeo and Juliet
ISBN 0-14-071484-7

The Sonnets
ISBN 0-14-071453-7

The Taming of the Shrew
ISBN 0-14-071451-0

The Tempest
ISBN 0-14-071485-5

Timon of Athens
ISBN 0-14-071487-1

Titus Andronicus
ISBN 0-14-071491-X

Troilus and Cressida
ISBN 0-14-071486-3

Twelfth Night
ISBN 0-14-071489-8

The Two Gentlemen of Verona
ISBN 0-14-071461-8

The Winter's Tale
ISBN 0-14-071488-X